Jack C. Richards & Chuck Sandy

Passages

Third Edition

Salina Alves de Lima
September, 2015

Workbook 2

CAMBRIDGE
UNIVERSITY PRESS

CAMBRIDGE
UNIVERSITY PRESS

32 Avenue of the Americas, New York, NY 10013-2473, USA

Cambridge University Press is part of the University of Cambridge.

It furthers the University's mission by disseminating knowledge in the pursuit of education, learning and research at the highest international levels of excellence.

www.cambridge.org
Information on this title: www.cambridge.org/9781107627260

© Cambridge University Press 2015

This publication is in copyright. Subject to statutory exception and to the provisions of relevant collective licensing agreements, no reproduction of any part may take place without the written permission of Cambridge University Press.

First published 1998
Second edition 2008
Reprinted 2015

Printed in Mexico by Editorial Impresora Apolo, S.A. de C.V.

A catalog record for this publication is available from the British Library.

ISBN 978-1-107-62707-9 Student's Book 2
ISBN 978-1-107-62714-7 Student's Book 2A
ISBN 978-1-107-62715-4 Student's Book 2B
ISBN 978-1-107-62726-0 Workbook 2
ISBN 978-1-107-62734-5 Workbook 2A
ISBN 978-1-107-62780-2 Workbook 2B
ISBN 978-1-107-62766-6 Teacher's Edition 2 with Assessment Audio CD/CD-ROM
ISBN 978-1-107-62749-9 Class Audio 2 CDs
ISBN 978-1-107-62773-4 Full Contact 2
ISBN 978-1-107-62774-1 Full Contact 2A
ISBN 978-1-107-62777-2 Full Contact 2B
ISBN 978-1-107-62764-2 DVD 2
ISBN 978-1-107-68650-2 Presentation Plus 2

Additional resources for this publication at www.cambridge.org/passages

Cambridge University Press has no responsibility for the persistence or accuracy of URLs for external or third-party internet websites referred to in this publication, and does not guarantee that any content on such websites is, or will remain, accurate or appropriate. Information regarding prices, travel timetables, and other factual information given in this work is correct at the time of first printing but Cambridge University Press does not guarantee the accuracy of such information thereafter.

Book design: Q2A / Bill Smith
Art direction, layout services and photo research: Tighe Publishing Services

Contents

Credits

Illustration credits

Jo Goodberry: 12
Paul Hostetler: 19, 26, 38, 49
Kim Johnson: 10, 31, 36, 55, 64
Dan McGeehan: 17, 18, 48
Koren Shadmi: 3, 20, 34, 43, 61
James Yamasaki: 41, 68

Photography credits

1 ©Photodisc/Thinkstock; **4** (*left to right*) ©Blend Images/Alamy, ©arek_malang/Shutterstock, ©Suprijono Suharjoto/Thinkstock; **5** (*clockwise from center left*) ©Fuse/Thinkstock, ©Michael Simons/Alamy, ©pcruciatti /Shutterstock, ©Dmitriy Shironosov/Thinkstock; **6** ©Catherine Yeulet/Thinkstock; **7** ©Fuse/Thinkstock; **8** ©crystalfoto/Shutterstock; **13** ©ID1974/Shutterstock; **14** (*top to bottom*) ©Olena Mykhaylova/iStock/Thinkstock, ©Oleksiy Mark/Thinkstock; **15** ©Stocktrek Images/Getty Images; **21** ©Flirt/SuperStock; **22** ©Photononstop/SuperStock; **23** ©BananaStock/Thinkstock; **24** ©ollyy/Shutterstock; **25** ©Khakimullin Aleksandr/Shutterstock; **27** (*top to bottom*) ©Vuk Vukmirovic/iStock/Thinkstock, ©Moviestore Collection Ltd/Alamy; **28** ©NBC/Getty Images; **30** ©CBS Photo Archive/Getty Images; **32** ©Larry Busacca/TAS/Getty Images; **35** ©Creatas/Getty Images/Thinkstock; **39** ©Cusp/SuperStock; **40** ©Tammy Hanratty/MediaBakery; **42** ©Photoshot/Hulton/Getty Images; **45** (*top to bottom*) ©Sergey Nivens/Shutterstock, ©iStock/franckreporter, ©iStock/MachineHeadz; **47** (*left to right, top to bottom*) ©Dean Bertoncelj/iStock/Thinkstock, ©Universal/Courtesy: Everett Collection, ©Kylie McLaughlin/Lonely Planet Images/Getty Images, ©MariusdeGraf/Shutterstock, ©Blend Images/Masterfile, ©Gao lin hk/Imaginechina/AP Images; **50** (*left to right, top to bottom*) ©MustafaNC/Shutterstock, ©Dmitry Zinovyev/Shutterstock, ©e2dan/Shutterstock, ©Reinhold Leitner/Shutterstock, ©Reddogs/Shutterstock, ©Nailia Schwarz/Shutterstock, ©Sergey Goruppa/Shutterstock, ©Wendy Kaveney Photography/Shutterstock, ©Donovan van Staden/Shutterstock, ©Nantawat Chotsuwan/Shutterstock, ©Steve Byland/istock/Thinkstock, ©iStock/Sergey Goruppa; **52** ©KidStock/Blend Images/Corbis; **53** (*top to bottom*) ©Gary Crabbe/Enlightened Images/Alamy, ©Falk Kienas/istock/Thinkstock; **54** ©Eric Isselée/Thinkstock; **57** ©E+/MachineHeadz/Getty Images; **59** ©Assembly/Media Bakery; **62** (*left to right, top to bottom*) ©Pressmaster/Shutterstock, ©Olga Danylenko/Shutterstock, ©iStock/btrenkel, ©Stockbyte/Thinkstock, ©Graham Oliver/Media Bakery, ©Andrey Yurlov/Shutterstock; **63** © INTERFOTO/Alamy; **65** ©Jon Kopaloff/FilmMagic/Getty Images; **66** ©ZUMA Press, Inc./Alamy; **71** ©Goodluz/Shutterstock; **Back cover:** (*clockwise from top center*) ©Leszek Bogdewicz/Shutterstock, ©Wavebreak Media/Thinkstock, ©Blend Images/Alamy, ©limpido/Shutterstock

Text credits

The authors and publishers acknowledge the following sources of copyright material and are grateful for the permissions granted. While every effort has been made, it has not always been possible to identify the sources of all the material used, or to trace all copyright holders. If any omissions are brought to our notice, we will be happy to include the appropriate acknowledgments on reprinting.

12 Adapted from "Decoding Body Language," by John Mole, 1999, http://www.johnmole.com. Reproduced with permission; **18** Adapted from "How Artificial Intelligence is Changing Our Lives," by Gregory M. Lamb. Adapted with permission from the September 16, 2012 issue of *The Christian Science Monitor*. Copyright © 2012 The Christian Science Monitor, www.CSMonitor.com; **24** Adapted from "Rumor Detectives: True Story or Online Hoax?" by David Hochman, *Reader's Digest*, April 2009. Reprinted with permission from Reader's Digest. Copyright © 2009 by The Reader's Digest Association, Inc.; **30** Adapted from an NPR news report titled "Is The 'CSI Effect' Influencing Courtrooms?" by Arun Rath, originally published on NPR.org on February 5, 2011 and used with the permission of NPR. Copyright © 2011 National Public Radio, Inc. Any unauthorized duplication is strictly prohibited; **36** Adapted from "Study Suggests Music May Someday Help Repair Brain," by Robert Lee Hotz, *Los Angeles Times*, November 9, 1998. Copyright © 1998 Los Angeles Times. Reprinted with permission; **42** Adapted from "What's the Tipping Point?" by Malcolm Gladwell. Copyright © by Malcolm Gladwell. Reprinted by permission of the author; **48** Adapted from "Sensory Ploys and the Scent of Marketing," by Robert Budden, *Financial Times*, June 3, 2013. Copyright © The Financial Times Limited 2013. All Rights Reserved; **54** Adapted from "Fairy Tale Comes True," by Alexandar S. Dragicevic, *The Toronto Star*, July 23, 1998. Copyright © Associated Press; **60** Adapted from "Does the Language you Speak Change the Way You Think?" by Kevin Hartnett, *The Boston Globe*, February 27, 2013. Reproduced with permission of Kevin Hartnett; **66** Adapted from "Tiny Grants Keep 'Awesome' Ideas Coming," by Billy Baker, *The Boston Globe*, October 10, 2011. Copyright © 2011 Boston Globe. All rights reserved. Used by permission and protected by the Copyright Laws of the United States. The printing, copying, redistribution, or retransmission of this Content without express written permission is prohibited; **72** Adapted from "The Twelve Attributes of a Truly Great Place to Work," by Tony Schwartz, *Harvard Business Review*, September 19, 2011. Reproduced with permission.

1 RELATIONSHIPS

LESSON A ▶ *The best of friends*

1 GRAMMAR

Read this paragraph from a blog post about friendship. Find the phrasal verbs and write them in the correct columns in the chart.

> I have a lot of friends, but my best friend is Anna. She is one of those great friends you come by only once in a while. Anna knows how to cheer me up when I'm feeling bad, and she brings out the best in me when I'm feeling happy. Whenever I run into a problem, she always has great advice, and she usually helps me solve it. She never puts me down when I do something silly or embarrassing. I guess the thing I like best about Anna is that I can open up to her and talk about anything, like bad grades in school or family problems. I would never turn her down if she needed my help. I would stand up for her in just about any situation. I really hope that we don't drift apart in the future. I don't think I could do without her friendship!

Separable	Inseparable	Three-word verbs	Intransitive
	come by		

2 VOCABULARY

Choose the words that best complete the sentences.

1. When Mike's and Ed's ideas about art *clash* / *admire*, they argue.

2. My sister is a truly *admirable* / *beneficial* person. She works two jobs, goes to school at night, and still has time to help me with my problems.

3. Jon and Scott *empathize* / *harmonize* well as a team since they have similar working styles.

4. Kim and Emily have a truly *clashing* / *enduring* relationship. They have been best friends for more than 10 years.

5. Catherine has *benefited* / *endured* a lot from living with her grandmother, who is very understanding and a great listener.

6. Lara is good with teenagers. She is very *empathetic* / *harmonious*, really listening to their problems and helping them find their own solutions.

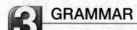

3 GRAMMAR

Complete these conversations with the correct form of the phrasal verbs in the box.
Use an object pronoun where needed.

| cheer (someone) up | drift apart | stand up for |
| do without | run into | turn (someone) down |

1. A: I'm surprised that Tom didn't support what you said in the meeting.
   I thought he agreed with you.
   B: He does agree with me, but he was afraid of what our boss would say.
   I can't believe he didn't _____ *stand up for* _____ me!

2. A: What's wrong with Carmen? She looks so sad.
   B: I'm not sure. Let's ask her to go to lunch with us. Maybe we can
   _____.

3. A: Did Eric ask you to present your work at the conference next week?
   B: Yes, he did, but I _____ because I have other
   things to take care of at work.

4. A: Sam isn't serious about anything. I think we could really
   _____ him on our team.
   B: I agree. Let's talk to the others about it and make a decision.

5. A: Have you seen Yuki lately?
   B: Actually, I _____ her when I was downtown today.

6. A: Is it true that you and Roger aren't in touch anymore?
   B: Yes, it is. We kind of _____ when I moved to Los Angeles.

4 GRAMMAR

Complete these sentences to make them true for you.

1. Nothing cheers me up as much as *going out to dinner with a few of my*
   good friends! _____

2. I like to hang on to friends who _____
   _____

3. When someone puts me down, I _____
   _____

4. I will stand up for anyone who _____
   _____

5. I can do without people who _____
   _____

6. I open up around people who _____
   _____

WRITING

A Read the thesis statements. Find the three best paragraph topics to support each one. Write the topics below the thesis statements.

Paragraph Topics

- ✔ Keep in touch through social media, video calls, and email.
- ✔ Be a person that your friend can trust.
- ✔ Join clubs and other organizations related to your interests or hobbies.
- ✔ Know when to give advice and when to keep silent.
- ✔ Sign up for a class, such as painting or cooking.
- ✔ Participate in community service activities, such as working with the elderly.
- ✔ Pay attention to what your friend thinks and feels.
- ✔ Get together and travel whenever possible.
- ✔ Send cards and presents for special occasions such as birthdays and holidays.

Thesis statements

1. Developing a friendship requires attention and work.

    Be a person that your friend can trust.

    _____

    _____

2. People living in big cities often have trouble making friends, but there are ways to solve this problem.

    _____

    _____

    _____

3. Maintaining a long-distance friendship is difficult, but it can be done.

    _____

    _____

    _____

B Write one additional topic for each thesis statement in part A.

1. _____

2. _____

3. _____

C Choose one of the thesis statements and write a composition. Use three paragraph topics that best support your thesis.

LESSON B ▶ *Make new friends, but keep the old . . .*

1 GRAMMAR

Read these online profiles. Underline the verb + gerund constructions, and circle the verb + infinitive constructions.

1 Naomi

My name is Naomi. I'm 30 years old, and I'm a teacher. I tend to be on the shy side, so I'm considering starting a book club so I can meet some new people. I plan to start this club as soon as possible, so email me if you're interested!

Naomi247@cup.org

2 Renee

I just moved here, and I'm looking for some new friends. I appreciate spending evenings at home cooking and listening to music. People say I tend to be kind of quiet, but I'm fun once you know more about me. If you enjoy sharing recipes, email me.

Renee8334@cup.org

3 Alex

I'm Alex Ramirez, an engineering student at National University. I really enjoy biking. Can I suggest starting a bikers' meet-up group? I'm considering entering a race, and therefore, I intend to start riding my bike every day. I hope others will join me!

alex.ramirez@cup.org

2 GRAMMAR

Complete the questions using the gerund or infinitive form of the verbs. Note that one of the constructions uses the passive voice. Then answer the questions and give reasons.

1. Do you get annoyed when friends ask _____*to borrow*_____ (borrow) your clothes?
   No, I don't get annoyed because I know my friends will return the clothes.

2. Would you give up _____ (practice) an instrument or sport if you got to spend more time with friends?

   _____

3. Would you refuse _____ (go out) with a friend if he or she wanted to see a movie you weren't interested in seeing?

   _____

4. Do you expect _____ (invite) every time your best friend goes out?

   _____

5. Which friend do you prefer _____ (hang out) with the most?

   _____

6. When a friend treats you to lunch, do you enjoy _____ (go) to a casual restaurant or a more formal one?

   _____

7. Would you continue _____ (talk) to a friend if he or she never answered your texts or emails?

   _____

VOCABULARY

Choose the words that best complete the sentences.

1. Maria and Emma (rekindled) / *resurfaced* their friendship after drifting apart from each other for many years.

2. Good friends are impossible to *replace* / *resurface*. They share so many of our memories.

3. Too much damage has been done to Al and Sam's friendship to *redefine* / *rebuild* it.

4. I can't *rehash* / *recall* the name of my tenth-grade English teacher.

5. Tim has *reconnected* / *redefined* his outlook on life. He's more optimistic now.

6. Don't bring that subject up again. I don't want to *rehash* / *rebuild* it with you.

7. After studying for the exam for two days, Cara *redefined* / *resurfaced* to eat dinner with her family.

8. I'm glad I came home for spring break. I've been *recalling* / *reconnecting* with friends that I haven't seen since last summer.

GRAMMAR

Imagine your friend is coming to visit you for the weekend. Write sentences describing some possible activities you can do together. Use the cues and the gerund or infinitive form of the verbs.

1. plan / take a walk somewhere nice

    We should plan to take a walk

    somewhere nice.

2. suggest / relax at a cozy café

    _____

    _____

3. consider / go to a club

    _____

    _____

4. prefer / get tickets to a concert

    _____

    _____

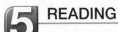

A Read the article. Find the words in boldface that match the definitions.

1. causes _____*spurs*_____
2. thin _____
3. annoying reminders _____
4. a good indication of _____
5. more commonly affected by _____
6. take care of and engage socially _____

Your FRIENDS & Your HEALTH «

"You're not what you eat – you're who you eat with," wrote *Scientific American*'s Christie Nicholson, reporting on research examining why our friends' weight influences our own. The study found that overweight students were more likely to lose weight if they hung out with **lean** friends – **a clear nod to** the influence of our social networks on our waistlines. But helping you lose weight isn't the only way your friends can affect you. Here are some other ways friends are good for our health:

FRIENDS GET YOU MOVING Research has found that something you might expect from your family – **nagging** – can actually work when it's coming from a pal pushing you to move more. Also, working out with a friend has the added benefit of keeping you committed to your workout plan. There's no rolling over to hit the snooze button on that early morning run if someone's waiting for you to show up!

FRIENDS KEEP YOU RELAXED Talking with friends really can help you get through troublesome times. Women in particular may be **predisposed to** the calming benefits of friendship. Researchers found that women release the hormone oxytocin when stressed, which encourages **"tend and befriend"** behavior, the *San Francisco Chronicle* reported. Chatting with friends when stressed **spurs** the release of more oxytocin, which can have a calming effect.

FRIENDS KEEP YOUR HEART HEALTHY Perhaps because they help us relax, friends are also good for the heart. Stronger social ties in general seem to lower blood pressure, which helps the heart. Married men, for example, seem to experience a particular boost in heart health, WebMD reported.

FRIENDS HELP YOU LIVE LONGER In an analysis of 148 studies, researchers found that people with stronger relationships had a 50 percent greater chance of long-term survival than those with weaker social networks. It's not quite as simple as connecting with friends and, poof, you're guaranteed to live to 100, but there is a significant body of research linking strong social ties to a longer lifespan.

B Choose the statements that are supported by information in the article.

☐ 1. Men don't seem to benefit from the relaxing effects of friendship.

☐ 2. The eating habits and lifestyle of our friends can have an influence on our own health.

☐ 3. Making plans to exercise with a friend increases the likelihood that you will.

☐ 4. Having strong social ties does not seem to have an effect on women's blood pressure.

☐ 5. Evidence suggests that strong social ties can lead to a longer life.

2 CLOTHES AND APPEARANCE

LESSON A ▶ *The way we dress*

1 GRAMMAR

Match the two parts of each sentence to tell the story of Mimi, a fashion designer.

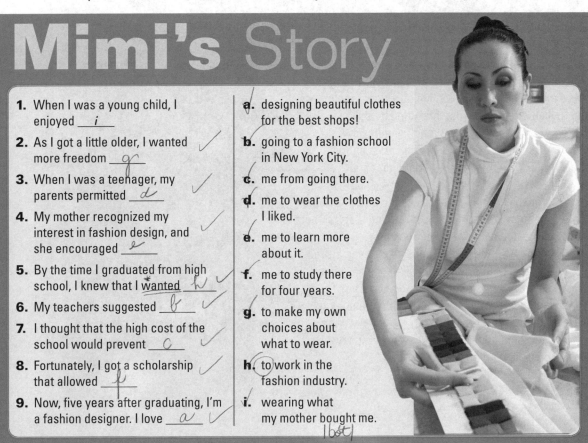

Mimi's Story

1. When I was a young child, I enjoyed ___i___
2. As I got a little older, I wanted more freedom ___g___
3. When I was a teenager, my parents permitted ___d___
4. My mother recognized my interest in fashion design, and she encouraged ___e___
5. By the time I graduated from high school, I knew that I wanted* ___h___
6. My teachers suggested ___b___
7. I thought that the high cost of the school would prevent ___c___
8. Fortunately, I got a scholarship that allowed ___f___
9. Now, five years after graduating, I'm a fashion designer. I love ___a___

a. designing beautiful clothes for the best shops!
b. going to a fashion school in New York City.
c. me from going there.
d. me to wear the clothes I liked.
e. me to learn more about it.
f. me to study there for four years.
g. to make my own choices about what to wear.
h. to work in the fashion industry.
i. wearing what my mother bought me. |bst|

* *want sempre precisa do to*

2 VOCABULARY

Choose the words that best complete the sentences.
→ *desuidado*

1. People read fashion magazines to learn about the *sloppy* / (stylish) new clothing for each season.
   |sloppy|
2. If you are planning to go to a fancy club, wear something (*chic* / *functional*. → *peculiar*
3. Marco's (*conservative*) / *quirky* suit was appropriate for his interview at the bank.
   |cuorquij|
4. Many teenagers think adults wear unimaginative, *fashionable* / (*stuffy*) clothing.
5. When I'm alone at home, I can wear *formal* / (*sloppy*) clothes if I want.
6. I can't understand why some people wear *retro* / *trendy* clothes from decades ago – they're so old-fashioned! → *na moda última moda*
7. When I'm gardening, I wear *flashy* / (*functional*) jeans and a T-shirt. → *chamativo*
8. Pop stars often wear (*trendy*) / *frumpy* clothes on stage.

↳ *of a woman clothes* (*dowdy*) → *deselegante*
and old-fashioned

→ quando coloca muita coisa no mesmo lugar
→ ? abafado lugar

Verb + infinitive   or   Verb + gerund. { Enjoy
(to)   action (ing)   Consider
                                    Mind
                                    Miss

③ GRAMMAR Agree, Promise, Want, Plan

Read the blog post about clothes and fashion. Use the gerund or the infinitive form of the verbs in parentheses.

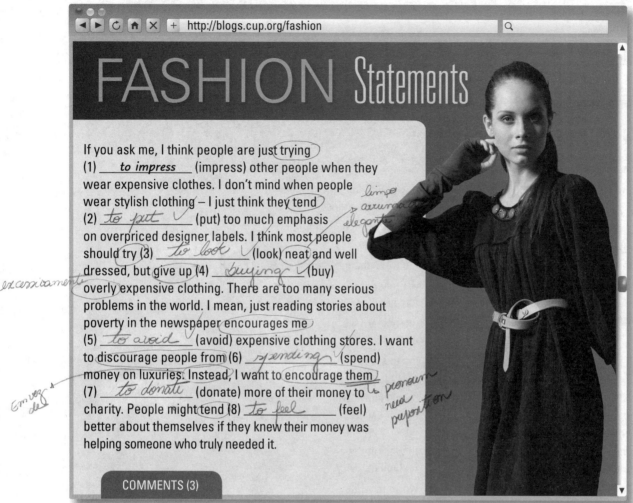

http://blogs.cup.org/fashion

FASHION Statements

If you ask me, I think people are just trying
(1) __to impress__ (impress) other people when they
wear expensive clothes. I don't mind when people
wear stylish clothing – I just think they tend
(2) __to put__ (put) too much emphasis
on overpriced designer labels. I think most people
should try (3) __to look__ (look) neat and well
dressed, but give up (4) __buying__ (buy)
overly expensive clothing. There are too many serious
problems in the world. I mean, just reading stories about
poverty in the newspaper encourages me
(5) __to avoid__ (avoid) expensive clothing stores. I want
to discourage people from (6) __spending__ (spend)
money on luxuries. Instead, I want to encourage them
(7) __to donate__ (donate) more of their money to
charity. People might tend (8) __to feel__ (feel)
better about themselves if they knew their money was
helping someone who truly needed it.

limpo
arrumado
elegante

excessivamente

Emveg des

pronoun
need
preposition

COMMENTS (3)

④ GRAMMAR

Complete these sentences to make them true for you. *pensar para / tieudar*

1. I don't mind wearing clothes that _are handed down to me from my brothers or cousins._

2. I hate to wear clothes that _are not comfortable._
   make me fell uncomfortable

3. I love to wear clothes that _express my personality._
   make me look thin.

4. When I'm shopping for clothes, I enjoy _looking for { deals / good prices and quality._

5. When getting dressed for a night out, I tend _to feel elegant or more trending._

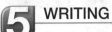

WRITING

A Underline the thesis statements in these introductory paragraphs. Then complete each paragraph that follows with examples supporting each thesis statement.

> *vestir x elegante*   *> desprezar*

There are many reasons for getting <u>dressed up.</u> Yet many of my friends seem to (despise) wearing anything but jeans and T-shirts. Personally, I look forward to opportunities to put on my best clothes and like to dress nicely for many different types of occasions.

> *agradavel*

There are many advantages to dressing (nicely.) For example, _you may have an unexpected dinner or meeting or date and you aren't well dressed._   *situation*

_____

_____

> *xenda*

Young people spend a significant portion of their (income) on the "right clothes." Following

> *o mais novo* *> esforço*

the (newest) (trends) in an (effort) to fit in can become an obsession, and keeping up with the

> *perseguir*

latest fashions can be an expensive (pursuit.) I feel that young people need to reject the pressure to dress stylishly.

> *consciente*

Young people should be (aware) that fashion magazines and blogs do not always set a good example. That is, _people don't have maturity enough to understant. Sometime they make mistakes such as drugs, alcohol, ..._

_____

_____

B Choose one of these topics to write about. Then choose one of the verbs to make the thesis statement express your point of view.

1. There (are) / aren't many advantages to dressing casually at work.
2. Students (should) / shouldn't be required to wear school uniforms.
3. People should / (shouldn't) be judged by what they wear.

C Make a list of examples that support your thesis statement.

_____

Everyone have the own opnion, style.

D Use your thesis statement and examples to write a composition containing an introductory paragraph and at least two supporting paragraphs.

GRAMMAR

Read the email and underline the cleft sentences.

root, parcel

To:	beth234@mail.cup.org
Subject:	Kyle's visit

Dear Beth,

Guess what! My brother Kyle visited me yesterday. I hadn't seen him in a year. <u>What I noticed first was the three inches he grew.</u> He looks so tall now!

He wanted to go out for lunch, so we went to my favorite café. We talked for a while. <u>What struck me most about him was how grown up he sounded.</u> *atingue* He told me that he's doing well in school and that he has a part-time job at a supermarket – and he's even been saving money for college.

After lunch, we walked through the park. Then he had to leave, but before he did, he gave me a big hug and promised to visit me again. <u>What I realized at the end of the visit was that I have a really terrific brother!</u>

Love, Erica

was past to be (is)

GRAMMAR

Read what each person thought about Gina Riccardi, a model who visited an advertising agency. Then complete the conversation using cleft sentences with *admired, liked, noticed,* or *struck me*.

Jin: She's as beautiful in person as she is in her ads.

Brian: She is gorgeous, but (1) *what I noticed first was how relaxed and friendly she seems*.

Dolores: That's true, but (2) *what struck me must was her eyes.* *is necessary article* How about you, Jin? *impressionante / belíssimo*

Jin: Yes, her eyes are stunning, but (3) *what I liked was (what) she did with her hair*

Ted: As for me, (4) *what admired was her beautiful voice.*

Brian: You're right. Her voice is very expressive. Actually, I hear she's about to act in her first movie.

3 VOCABULARY

Choose the words in the box that best complete the sentences.

arrogant	eccentric	intense	sympathetic
dignified	intellectual	sinister	trustworthy

1. People think Ryan is strange and _____*eccentric*_____ because he lives with 12 cats.

2. The villain was so ____*sinistre*____ that I shivered with fear. *extremecu* ✓

3. Jonathan is so ____*arrogant*____. He thinks he's better than everyone in the office. ✓

4. If you need a ____*sympathetic*____ person to talk to, try Maya. She's very understanding. ✓

5. Don't count on David to keep any secrets. He's not very ____*trustworthy*____. ✓

6. Jiro was very ____*intense*____ during the debate. He clearly has strong opinions about the topic! ✓

7. Keri is so ____*intellectual*____. She could be a college professor! *permonecu* ✓

8. Despite all the reporters shouting questions at her, the politician remained calm and ____*dignified*____, not showing that she was upset at all. *Apesar de* ✓ *↳ chateado*

4 GRAMMAR

Imagine you are moving to a town where you don't know anyone. What personal characteristics do you look for in potential friends? Use your own ideas to complete these sentences.

1. What I look for in a friend is _a sincere interest in other people and_
a sympathetic personality.

2. What I think is most important is _the person is dignified and_ ✓
trustworthy.

3. What I probably notice first is _the sympathy_ ✓

4. What I pay attention to is _the behavior_ ✓

5. What I try to find out about a new friend first is _a trustworthy friend._ ✓ *descobrir*

6. What I think is least important is _financial condition._ *status* ✓
where they from.

5 READING

A Read the article quickly. Which of these behaviors apply to each body language type?

	Willing to listen	Not willing to listen	Engaged in conversation	Not engaged in conversation
1. responsive	☑	☐	☑	☐
2. reflective	☑	☐	☐	☑
3. combative	☐	☑	☑	☐
4. fugitive	☐	☑	☐	☑

Understanding BODY LANGUAGE

em direção *inclinar*

In European and North American cultures, body language behaviors can be divided into two groups: open/closed and forward/back.

Open/closed postures are the easiest to recognize. People are open to messages when they show open hands, face you fully, and have both feet on the ground. This indicates that they are willing to listen to what you have to say, even if they are disagreeing with you. When people are closed to messages, they have their arms folded or their legs crossed, and they may turn their bodies away. What this body language usually means is that people are rejecting your message.

mais fácil *totalmente* *disposto*

Forward/back behavior reveals an active or a passive reaction to what is being said. If people lean forward with their bodies toward you, they are actively engaged in your message. They may be accepting or rejecting it, but their minds are on what you are saying. On the other hand, if people lean back in their chairs or look away from you, or perform activities such as drawing or cleaning their eyeglasses, you know that they are either passively taking in your message or that they are ignoring it. In either case, they are not very engaged in the conversation.

The chart below shows how these types of body language can suggest the general mental state of the listener.

OPEN

RESPONSIVE: The person is willing to listen to you (open) and wants to participate in the conversation (forward).

REFLECTIVE: The person is willing to listen (open) but not to share his or her opinion (back). He or she wants more time to think.

FORWARD ←——————→ BACK

COMBATIVE: There is risk of an argument. The person is engaged in the conversation (forward) but rejects your message (closed).

FUGITIVE: The person is trying to avoid the conversation. He or she does not want to be a part of the conversation (back) and is rejecting your message (closed).

CLOSED

B Write the body language type under each picture.

responsive
reflective
combative
fugitive

1. _Combative_ / _Fugitive_   2. _reflective_   3. _responsive_   4. _fugitive_ / _Combative_

12 **UNIT 2** Clothes and appearance

3 SCIENCE AND TECHNOLOGY

LESSON A ▶ *Good science, bad science*

1 GRAMMAR

Choose the sentences that use articles incorrectly, and then rewrite them.

☑ 1. For some people, using an abacus is an alternative to using calculator.
   For some people, using an abacus is an
   alternative to using a calculator.

☐ 2. Abacus is the earliest form of mechanical computing.
   _____

☐ 3. The abacus was invented more than 4,000 years ago.
   _____

☐ 4. It consists of wires strung across wooden frame.
   _____

☐ 5. An abacus can have up to 13 wires. On wires are beads, which represent units.
   _____

☐ 6. Calculations are made by moving the beads up and down the wires.
   _____

☐ 7. Skilled operator can make calculations on it very quickly.
   _____

2 VOCABULARY

Choose the words in the box that best complete the sentences.

audacious	frivolous	problematic	unethical
confidential	hazardous	prudent	

1. Some people consider cosmetic surgery harmful and a/an _____*frivolous*_____ waste of money when not done for serious health reasons.

2. Curing cancer is still a/an _____ issue for scientists.

3. In some countries, doctors must keep medical records _____. They are forbidden to share information, even with family members.

4. Some people get sick due to improper storage or disposal of _____ materials like chemicals and poisons.

5. It's illegal and _____ to download music without permission.

6. It would take _____ actions to go against our boss's plans.

7. It would be _____ to review the contract with a lawyer before signing it. Don't put yourself at risk by making a bad deal.

3 GRAMMAR

Complete the text with *a*, *an*, or *the*. Write an *X* where an article is not required.

Digital **Cameras**

Since the early 1990s, (1) ___the___ digital camera has changed the way we take (2) _____ pictures.

Traditional film cameras worked by focusing (3) _____ image onto light-sensitive film in the camera. To see the pictures, you had to send (4) _____ film to (5) _____ company that processed it. This was (6) _____ process that could take several hours.

Of course, digital cameras don't use film. Rather, they convert light entering the camera into (7) _____ information that can be read by (8) _____ computer. One advantage of this process is that you can see (9) _____ images immediately.

Another advantage is that you can delete (10) _____ pictures you don't like, and you can improve (11) _____ image by using special software. Of course, this can be (12) _____ disadvantage, too, since it's nearly impossible to tell just from looking whether a photo is real or not.

4 GRAMMAR

Write a sentence about each topic.

- the most helpful kind of technology
- the trendiest product on the market
- the silliest invention
- a medical cure I'd like to see discovered
- the most interesting website

1. *I think the most helpful kind of technology is the solar panel, which can provide electricity without producing much harmful waste.*

2. _____

   _____

3. _____

   _____

4. _____

   _____

5. _____

   _____

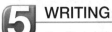

A Read the article. Underline the main information in each paragraph that would belong in a summary.

ASTEROID MINING

One day in the not-so-distant future, small robotic spaceships will search the inner solar system mapping asteroids and determining which to harvest. Those asteroids containing valuable resources like iron, nickel, hydrogen, and reusable water will then be mined by larger robotic spacecrafts or turned into space-based manufacturing centers.

Robotically controlled factories built on asteroids will turn space rock water into rocket fuel and asteroid metals into everything needed for space-based manufacturing. Given the possibly endless supply of resource-rich asteroids, the pioneers of asteroid mining will become incredibly wealthy as they lead us into a new age of space development. At least, that's the plan.

Although it may sound like science fiction, big investors are already taking such ideas seriously enough to put substantial money into asteroid mining and space exploration companies. NASA, the U.S. space agency, is enthusiastic. In fact,

NASA sees these plans as the first step toward colonizing space. By locating manufacturing facilities and rocket fueling stations on asteroids already in space, costs will be reduced and long journeys into space will become possible. This will make human colonization of other parts of the solar system a real possibility.

Before we get too excited, though, it's important to remember that most of the technology needed to mine asteroids and build orbital factories doesn't exist yet. Still, early investors and the companies they're investing in believe they will be successful and that along the way the asteroid-mining technologies they develop will help bring about a new age.

B Choose the sentence in each pair that could belong in a summary of the article.

1. ☐ There is a great deal of serious interest in mining asteroids for their valuable resources.

   ☐ Many asteroids contain valuable resources such as iron and nickel.

2. ☐ NASA feels asteroid mining could make space colonization possible.

   ☐ Asteroid mining could lead to a new era of space exploration and colonization.

C Now, write a summary of the article by rewriting the main points in your own words.

_____

_____

_____

_____

_____

_____

_____

_____

_____

_____

1 GRAMMAR

Read the sentences. Choose whether the *-ing* clause implies actions that happened at the same time, at a different time, or for a reason. Sometimes more than one answer is possible.

	Same time	Different time	Reason
1. Having recently learned how to text, my grandmother now sends me several messages a day!	☐	☑	☑
2. Being a prudent consumer, I did some research before I bought my laptop.	☐	☐	☑ ✓
3. While going to the birthday party, I got lost.	☑	☐	☐ ✓
4. Having lost my ATM card, I can't withdraw money from an ATM.	☐	☑	☑ ✓
5. Having downloaded a new video calling app, I can call friends anywhere in the world for free.	☐	☑	☑ ✓
6. Zoe is in her room watching movies on her tablet.	☑	☐	☐ ✓
7. Having had trouble programming my home security system, I now ask my wife to program it for us.	☐	☑	☑ ✓

2 GRAMMAR

Write sentences using the (cues) and an *-ing* clause.

1. *Same time:* Lily / break her digital camera / take a picture

   Lily broke her digital camera taking a picture.

   Taking a picture, Lily broke her digital camera.

2. *Different time:* Diego / watch a show about alternative energy / buy an electric car

   Having watched a show about alternative energy bought an electric car. ✓

3. *Reason:* Bella / be a resourceful person / build her own computer

   Being a resourceful person, Bella built her own computer. ✓

4. *Different time:* Dan / injure his arm / receive a bone scan

   Having injured his arm Dan received a bone scan. ✓

5. *Same time:* Celia / be in her car / listen to satellite radio

   Celia is in her car listening to satellite radio. ✓

6. *Reason:* Ken / be an eco-conscious person / always recycles his old electronics

   Being an eco-conscious person, Ken always recycles his old electronics ✓

3 VOCABULARY

Match the clauses to make logical sentences.

1. Anita is (fed up) with Tyler ___c___
2. Children are reliant on their parents ___f___
3. Julia is grateful for all the help ___a___
4. Make sure you are familiar with ___h___
5. I'm curious about ___g___
6. People are intimidated by George, ___e___
7. Gwen is so crazy about cooking ___d___
8. I've been suspicious of Ryan ___b___

a. she got from friends while she was ill.
b. ever since I saw him holding my phone.
c. because he asks too many questions.
d. that she opened her own restaurant.
e. but he's actually nicer than he looks!
f. to feed, shelter, and clothe them until they're grown.
g. what happens next on my favorite TV show.
h. the program before using it in your next presentation.

4 GRAMMAR

Have you had good or bad experiences doing the activities in the box or similar activities using technology? Write sentences about your experience using *-ing* clauses.

> ✓ using a video streaming service
> learning how to use a new cell phone
> creating a social networking profile
> shopping online

1. *Having signed up for a new video streaming service, I realized it didn't offer all the movies I wanted to see.*

2. _____

3. _____

4. _____

A What does *mundanely ubiquitous* mean? Read the article and choose the answer.

☐ unsurprisingly common ☐ amazingly rare

ARTIFICIAL INTELLIGENCE
IN OUR LIVES

From the Curiosity space probe that landed on Mars without human help, to the cars whose dashboards we can now talk to, to smartphones that talk back to us, so-called artificial intelligence (AI) is changing our lives – sometimes in ways that are obvious and visible, but often in subtle and invisible forms.

AI is making Internet searches quicker, translating texts from one language to another, and recommending a better route through traffic. It helps detect fraudulent patterns in credit-card searches and tells us when we've crossed over the center line while driving. Even your toaster is about to join the AI revolution. You'll put a bagel in it, take a picture with your smartphone, and the phone will send the toaster all the information it needs to brown the bread perfectly.

In a sense, AI has become almost **mundanely ubiquitous,** from the intelligent sensors that adjust the settings in digital cameras, to the heat and humidity probes in dryers, to the automatic parking feature in cars. And more applications for AI are coming out of labs and laptops by the hour. "It's an exciting world," says Colin Angle, cofounder of a company that has created a robotic vacuum cleaner that uses AI to navigate its way around furniture.

What may be most surprising about AI today, in fact, is how little amazement it creates. Perhaps science-fiction stories with humanlike androids – from the charming Data in *Star Trek*, to the obedient C-3PO in *Star Wars*, to the sinister Terminator in the similarly named series of movies – have raised unrealistic expectations. Or maybe human nature just doesn't stay amazed for long.

"Today's mind-popping, eye-popping technology in 18 months will be as blasé and old as a 1980s pair of double-knit trousers," says Paul Saffo, who analyzes trends to predict the future. "Our expectations are a moving target." If voice-recognition programs in smartphones had come out in 1980, "it would have been the most astonishing, breathtaking thing," he says. But by the time they arrived, "we were so used to other things going on we said, 'Oh, yeah, no big deal.' Technology goes from magic to invisible-and-taken-for-granted in about two nanoseconds."

B For each pair of sentences, choose the one the author would agree with.

1. ☐ a. AI has become so integrated into technology that most people are unaware of it.
   ☐ b. AI is making some aspects of daily life more complicated than necessary.

2. ☐ a. People are surprised that AI is even better than their expectations from movies.
   ☐ b. People aren't amazed by AI because of their high expectations from movies.

3. ☐ a. Technology advances so quickly that it creates astonishment.
   ☐ b. Technology advances so rapidly that people don't stay impressed by it for long.

4. ☐ a. It's likely we'll quickly see an increasing number of new applications for AI.
   ☐ b. It's unlikely that there will be many new developments in AI.

SUPERSTITIONS AND BELIEFS

LESSON A ▶ *Superstitions*

1 VOCABULARY

Match the phrases to make logical sentences.

1. I got into the best dorm on campus due to the __e__
2. Muriel had never bowled before, so her high score was ____
3. I tried to get tickets to the play, but I couldn't. I was ____
4. Before Max went off to college, I wished him the ____
5. Celia drives too fast. One day she's going to have an accident. I wish she wouldn't ____
6. I was hoping to get more information about the job, but ____
7. Jim's car was broken into twice in one week. He's had some really ____

a. push her luck.
b. bad luck.
c. best of luck.
d. out of luck.
e. luck of the draw.
f. beginner's luck.
g. no such luck.

2 GRAMMAR

Underline the reporting clauses in this passage.

Fact OR Fiction?

   Some ideas have been repeated so often that we just accept them as facts. <u>When someone asserts that</u> you can see the Great Wall of China from outer space, do we ask for proof? Probably not. But if you speak to anyone who's looked closely at photos of the earth taken from the moon, they'll sometimes admit that they can't find a trace of the Great Wall. And if people argue that you can badly hurt someone with a coin dropped from a very tall structure, we assume it must be true. Others have claimed that it's true many times before, right? However, experts agree that there's really no need to worry, and they report that a dropped coin could not reach a high enough speed to cause any real damage. One more case: Do you ever doubt that we, as humans, have only five senses? Not likely. Yet, apart from sight, smell, taste, and so on, some scientists explain that many other senses are in play: balance, movement, time, and hunger among them. However, there isn't much agreement about the total number, so maybe we should accept that there are five basic senses and leave the rest open to <u>Continue</u> . . .

3 GRAMMAR

Combine each pair of sentences using the words in parentheses.

1. As a child, I believed some strange things. A monster was living under my bed. (believe)

   As a child, I _____*believed (that)*_____ a monster _*was living under my bed*_.

2. To keep the monster away, I had to do certain things. I had to adjust the covers over me. (feel)

   To keep the monster away, I _____
   I _____.

3. I needed extra protection. My teddy bear would help me. (assume)

   I _____ my teddy bear _____.

4. I was fairly sure of one thing. My parents wouldn't believe me. (doubt)

   I _____ my parents _____.

4 GRAMMAR

Use the verbs in parentheses to explain what you think these people would do in the following situations.

1. Anna's friend won't travel on Friday the 13th because he considers it to be an unlucky day. Anna disagrees. How do you think Anna would reassure him? (explain)

   Anna would explain that Friday the 13th is just like any other day.

2. Luke's soccer teammate saw him rubbing a charm for good luck. How would Luke explain this? (admit)

   _____

3. Farah isn't superstitious, but her friend claims that following some superstitions brings good luck. How do you think Farah would respond? (argue)

   _____

 **WRITING**

A Read the text and answer the questions. Write the letter of the appropriate sentence.

1. Which sentence is the thesis statement? _____

2. Which sentence gives general examples? _____

3. Which sentence reflects the author's personal opinion about traditional beliefs? _____

4. Which sentence restates the thesis statement? _____

Traditional Beliefs

a Traditional beliefs are not the same as superstitions. They differ in that they supposedly transmit useful information from one generation to another. **b** For example, I'm sure most of us can remember our parents telling us to eat certain foods or to avoid specific behaviors. Is there wisdom in these teachings, or are they without value? **c** Some beliefs passed down through generations reflect current medical thinking, whereas others have not passed the test of time.

Did your mother ever tell you to eat your carrots because they're good for your eyes? Well, the truth is carrots contain high levels of vitamin A. Research has linked vitamin A deficiencies to vision problems in low light, so in this sense, eating plenty of carrots actually is good for your eyes. And is garlic really good for you? It turns out that it is. Eating garlic on a regular basis can reduce the risk of serious illness and detoxify the body. How about chicken soup? We now understand that chicken contains an amino acid that is similar to a drug often prescribed for people with respiratory infections.

Unfortunately, not all of mom's advice has withstood medical inquiry. For example, generations of children have been told not to go swimming for an hour after eating. But research suggests that there is no danger in having lunch and then diving back into the ocean. Is chocolate really bad for you? Well, no, not if it's dark chocolate. Researchers now understand that dark chocolate contains enough antioxidants to make small amounts of it a healthy choice. Are fresh fruit juices really better for you than sodas? Well, yes and no. Fruit juices can contain as much sugar as soda, and both can contribute to weight gain and tooth decay. The best drink of all is simply water.

d Even though science can persuade us that some of our traditional beliefs don't hold water, there is still a lot of wisdom in the beliefs that have been handed down from generation to generation. **e** After all, much of this lore has been accumulated from thousands of years of trial-and-error experience in family healthcare. **f** We should respect this informal body of knowledge even as we search for clear scientific evidence to prove it to be true or false.

B Write a composition about traditional beliefs in your own culture. Include some you think are true and some you think are not true. Be sure to restate the thesis statement from your first paragraph in the last paragraph.

GRAMMAR

Read the article and underline the reporting verbs that are in the passive voice.

A Famous HOAX

On October 30, 1938, perhaps the most famous broadcast in the history of radio took place. Heard all over the United States, the broadcast reported that a spacecraft from Mars had landed in a small town in New Jersey. It <u>was said</u> that the Martians were attacking the surrounding area with a deadly "heat ray." Radio reporters also claimed that huge war machines had emerged from the spacecraft. After much destruction, it was announced that the Martians were dying. Specialists suggested that the Martians had no resistance to earth's infectious diseases.

Of course, this story was just a radio play, based on the novel *War of the Worlds* by H. G. Wells and directed and performed by Orson Welles. However, it is generally claimed that many people believed it, and it was reported that there was widespread panic throughout the country, especially in New Jersey. While it was not the intention of the broadcast to frighten people, its effects were widespread and dramatic. It has been suggested that Welles's broadcast offers many lessons about how the mass media can affect people in their daily lives.

Orson Welles

 VOCABULARY

Cross out the word that does not fit the meaning of the sentence.

1. It is *conceivable* / ~~*misleading*~~ / *plausible* that many lowland areas will be under water if the current trend in climate change continues.

2. Fad diets that promise you'll lose 10 pounds the first day sound *convincing* / *fishy* / *far-fetched* to me. There's no way you can lose 10 pounds in one day!

3. Beware of *dubious* / *phony* / *well-founded* emails that ask you to supply personal information like your credit card number or your salary.

4. Greta gave such a(n) *believable* / *convincing* / *iffy* performance in the play that I almost forgot she was acting!

5. Stephanie's blog is *misleading* / *fishy* / *believable*. Her profile says she's 24, but I know for a fact she's only 18.

6. That Carl is a chef seems *far-fetched* / *dubious* / *conceivable* to me. The food he cooked for dinner was awful.

7. I don't believe that "all-natural" foods are better for you. Show me a *plausible* / *dubious* / *well-founded* article that proves it, and then maybe I'll believe it.

8. When Kay told me she found a great used car online, it sounded *iffy* / *far-fetched* / *credible* to me. But the car is actually pretty nice!

3 GRAMMAR

Rewrite these sentences with the words in parentheses. Use a reporting clause in the passive with *it*.

1. More than two billion people use the Internet. (estimate)
   It is estimated (that) more than two billion people use the Internet.

2. Fingernails grow faster on the hand that you use the most. (report)
   _____

3. The oldest living tree on earth is nearly 5,000 years old. (say)
   _____

4. In a baby's first year of life, parents lose between 400 and 750 hours of sleep. (believe)
   _____

5. Items like plastic cups and bags take between 500 and 1,000 years to break down. (explain)
   _____

6. About 100 hairs fall from a person's head each day. (claim)
   _____

4 GRAMMAR

Use the cues to write sentences with a reporting clause in the passive.

1. say / 15 minutes of exercise per day / may extend your life by three years
   It is said (that) 15 minutes of exercise per
   day may extend your life by three years.

2. report / the average American child / watches 20,000 commercials each year
   _____
   _____

3. suggest / traditional treatments such as acupuncture / are effective
   _____
   _____

4. claim / a cure for certain types of cancer / will be found soon
   _____
   _____

5. believe / some animals / can predict earthquakes
   _____
   _____

A Read the article quickly to find the answers to these questions.

1. When did the Mikkelsons begin Snopes.com? _____

2. How many people visit the website each month? _____

3. What is the mission of Snopes.com? _____

RUMOR DETECTIVES

A few years ago, a woman and her husband were coming home from a ski trip when they spotted a disabled car on the side of the road. It was raining, and the driver looked distressed, so they stopped and helped him fix his flat tire. The man was extremely grateful but didn't have any cash to reward them, so he took down their personal information. A week later, the couple got a call from their bank saying their mortgage had been paid and $10,000 deposited into their account by an appreciative Bill Gates.

"Ah, the grateful millionaire," says Barbara Mikkelson with a satisfied grin.

Barbara and her husband, David, run Snopes.com, the Internet's preeminent resource for verifying and debunking rumors, ridiculous claims, and email chain letters. Whether it's an urban legend like the Gates story, an overblown warning about the latest computer virus, or that bizarre photo circulating of "Hercules, the world's biggest dog," chances are Snopes has checked it out and rated it as "true," "false," or "undetermined."

What began in 1995 as a hobby for a pair of amateur folklorists has grown into one of the Internet's most trusted authorities – and a full-time profession for the Mikkelsons. Each month, millions of people visit Snopes.com. Even the word *Snopes* has gone viral – as in, "Why didn't you Snopes that junk before forwarding it to your entire email list?"

"It's not easy to find out if these things are true or not, so people turn to us," David says.

A passion for nosing around is what brought the Mikkelsons together, and it's still their prime motivation, though their work is more than just a labor of love. The couple now earns a "very healthy" income, David says, from advertising on the site.

Though the Mikkelsons are established figures on the Web, they still prefer old-fashioned research – scouring vintage catalogs, thumbing through four newspapers a day – over finding quick answers online. David admits, however, that he might use Google or Wikipedia as a starting point.

B Are these statements true (*T*), false (*F*), or is the information not given (*NG*) in the article? Write the correct letters.

_____ 1. The Mikkelsons are now millionaires because of their work on Snopes.com.

_____ 2. Snopes.com gets hundreds of stories a day that are as far-fetched as "the grateful millionaire" one.

_____ 3. The Mikkelsons never resort to using online sources to check dubious facts.

_____ 4. The word *Snopes* is sometimes used as a verb by people familiar with the site.

_____ 5. Snopes receives income from ads placed by major international corporations.

5 MOVIES AND TELEVISION

LESSON A ▶ *Movies*

VOCABULARY

Choose the words that best complete the sentences.

1. I love movies that are so *predictable* / *riveting* that you completely lose track of the time.

2. The last movie I saw wasn't original at all. In fact, it seemed pretty *formulaic* / *touching* to me.

3. The critics were disappointed with the director's new film. They said his work was unoriginal and *moving* / *mediocre*.

4. The heartbreaking relationship between the two main characters in this movie is beautiful and *predictable* / *touching*.

5. That movie was so *clichéd* / *engrossing* that I honestly forgot I was in my living room.

6. After seeing the *inspiring* / *predictable* story of a woman who set up an elephant rescue organization, I decided to volunteer at an animal shelter.

GRAMMAR

Underline the sentence adverbs in these conversations. Then write them in the chart below.

1. Jack: I don't trust all the facts in this documentary about Coco Chanel.
   Lisa: I don't agree. The writer clearly did his research and interviewed many people who knew her.

2. Jill: When is your new film coming out?
   Fei: Apparently in May, but there will be a private viewing in April.

3. Aaron: I wanted to see the new documentary about a homeless family, but it isn't playing anywhere.
   Emma: Haven't you heard? It was removed from the theaters. Supposedly, the director used footage of certain people without asking permission, and now there's a lawsuit.

4. Kurt: I'm surprised. That new action movie was so dull!
   Teresa: I know. The director probably thinks he doesn't need to try very hard after so many successful movies.

5. Josh: This is the third science fiction movie I've seen this month!
   Tara: Obviously, you really like that kind of movie.

6. Kazuo: This director's films are so funny!
   Julie: Yes, but unquestionably, there's a lot of deep emotion in them as well.

Certainty	Less certainty	Possibility and probability
clearly		

3 GRAMMAR

Rewrite these sentences using the sentence adverbs in parentheses.

1. That famous Dutch actor is going to direct a movie. (apparently)

   Apparently, that famous Dutch actor is going to direct a movie.
   That famous Dutch actor is apparently going to direct a movie.

2. Some movie studios are not interested in good acting as much as extreme action. (frankly)

   _____

3. This is a magazine for anyone with a very strong interest in cinema. (definitely)

   _____

4. There would be more interest in historical movies if they received more publicity. (probably)

   _____

5. Because of a lack of funding, fewer independent films will be made this year. (potentially)

   _____

4 GRAMMAR

How does watching movies in theaters compare with watching movies at home?
Write sentences using the adverbs provided.

1. _Watching a movie at home_ is clearly _more comfortable than watching a movie_
   in a theater.

2. _____ is potentially _____

   _____

3. Overall, _____

   _____

4. _____ unquestionably the most _____

   _____

5. Unfortunately, _____

   _____

5 WRITING

A Choose either a comedy or a documentary that you are familiar with, and write a review of the movie you have chosen. Your review should answer the following questions.

Documentary

1. What is the title of the documentary?

2. What is the documentary mainly about?

3. What is the primary purpose of the documentary? Does it try to explain, persuade, or something else?

4. How successful is the documentary at achieving its purpose? Explain.

5. Which aspects of the documentary are especially memorable?

6. Would you recommend it to others? Why or why not?

Comedy

1. What is the title of the comedy?

2. Who are the actors, and what characters do they play?

3. What is the basic plot of the movie?

4. What are the best aspects of the movie? Explain.

5. Is the movie successful as a comedy? Why or why not?

6. Would you recommend it to others? Why or why not?

_____

_____

_____

_____

_____

_____

_____

_____

_____

_____

_____

_____

B Read your review again. Are there places where adding more details would make your writing better? If so, go back and add these details.

GRAMMAR

Complete the email with *so*, *such*, *so many*, *so few*, *so much*, or *so little*.

To: nataliem3@cup.com
Subject: House

Hey Natalie,

Have you ever seen the TV show *House*? The series ended a while ago, but it's
1 ___such___ a good show that I can't stop watching the reruns! It's about a cranky doctor
and his medical team who save the lives of patients with mysterious diseases. I usually
have **2** _____ time for TV that I skip most medical dramas. But this show isn't a typical
medical drama where doctors are compassionate and
caring. Dr. House is rude. In fact, he's **3** _____ rude
that his patients are often afraid of him. But he's also
4 _____ a brilliant doctor that everybody admires
him. He knows **5** _____ about rare diseases that
he's usually the only person who can cure these patients.
I had no idea there were **6** _____ different kinds
of illnesses. I think you'd like this show. There are
7 _____ good shows on TV these days that you'll
really appreciate this one.

Marcus

 VOCABULARY

Write the type of TV show next to its description.

cartoon	documentary	news program	sketch comedy show	sports program
cooking show	game show	sitcom	soap opera	talk show

___game show___ 1. Participants compete for money and prizes by answering
questions that an average fifth grade student would know.

_____ 2. The complicated lives of the wealthy Ramirez family are
dramatized daily.

_____ 3. Ann Brady reports on the top news stories of the day.

_____ 4. The Lakers take on the Suns in game three of the playoffs.

_____ 5. Ty Ott interviews actor Ash Lake and chef Ami Tran.

_____ 6. Astronaut Neil Armstrong's life is reviewed in this program.

_____ 7. A boy and his ladybug friend star in this animated kids' show.

_____ 8. Alice Lee stars in this funny half-hour show about high school.

_____ 9. To win, chefs live together and prepare dishes for celebrity judges.

_____ 10. Weekly guests star with the regular cast in a series of ridiculous
situations.

3 GRAMMAR

Write six logical sentences by choosing one word or phrase from each column.
Sometimes more than one answer is possible.

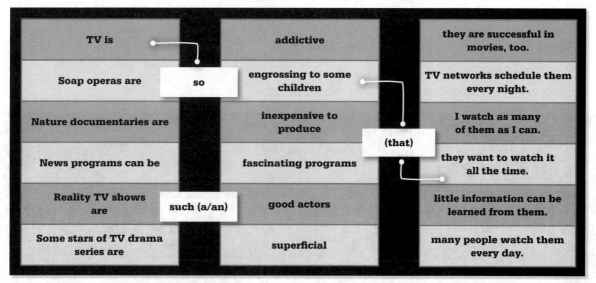

TV is	addictive	they are successful in movies, too.
Soap operas are **so**	engrossing to some children	TV networks schedule them every night.
Nature documentaries are	inexpensive to produce	I watch as many of them as I can.
News programs can be	fascinating programs **(that)**	they want to watch it all the time.
Reality TV shows are **such (a/an)**	good actors	little information can be learned from them.
Some stars of TV drama series are	superficial	many people watch them every day.

1. _TV is so engrossing to some children (that) they want to watch it all the time._
2. _____
3. _____
4. _____
5. _____
6. _____

4 GRAMMAR

Complete these sentences with your own ideas.

1. Some crime drama series can be so _violent_ that _I don't think children should_
   watch them.

2. There are so many _____ to watch this season that I
   _____

3. _____ is such a great actor that I _____
   _____

4. _____ night is such a good night to watch TV that _____
   _____

5. There are so few really funny shows on TV that I _____
   _____

6. Reality shows can be so _____ that I _____
   _____

READING

A Read the article. Find the words in boldface that match these definitions.

1. legal officials who accuse someone of a crime __*prosecutors*__
2. disqualify _____
3. scientific techniques used to investigate a crime _____
4. based on data rather than theory _____
5. groups of people who make a decision in a court case _____

IS THE "CSI EFFECT" INFLUENCING COURTROOMS?

The fictional forensic investigators in shows like *CSI: Crime Scene Investigation* put old-time detectives like Sherlock Holmes to shame. They can read a crime scene like it's a glossy magazine. But many **prosecutors** complain that shows like *CSI* make their job harder by creating the expectation that every trial must feature high-tech **forensic tests**. Some fear that when they don't show off *CSI*-style technology, **juries** might let criminals get away. It's termed the "*CSI* effect."

"I think that *CSI* has done some great things," says Mike Murphy, the coroner for Clark County, Nevada, whose office was the model for the original *CSI* show. "It's also caused some problems. And some of those problems are [that] people expect us to have DNA back in 20 minutes or that we're supposed to solve a crime in 60 minutes with three commercials. It doesn't happen that way," he says. Legal experts are concerned that juries may well be confusing fact with fiction.

However, Donald Shelton, the chief judge of Washtenaw County, Michigan, is skeptical. After realizing no **empirical** research on the *CSI* effect had been done, Shelton conducted a study showing that while jurors do expect to see scientific evidence in murder cases, their expectations have nothing to do with the TV shows they watch. They're more likely to be affected by the technology in their own pocket. "The more sophisticated [the] technological devices that jurors had, the higher their expectations for the prosecutors to present evidence," Shelton says.

Despite the lack of empirical evidence, lawyers, judges, and investigators act as if the *CSI* effect is real. In the U.S., some states now allow lawyers to **strike** potential jurors based on their TV habits. Judges are issuing instructions that warn juries about expecting too much scientific evidence based on what they see on TV. And in the field, Shelton says, investigators sometimes run useless tests just to show they went the extra *CSI* mile.

B Read these statements. Are they supported by the information in the article? Choose yes or no.

	Yes	No
1. Real or not, the *CSI* effect is clearly having an influence on courtrooms.	☐	☐
2. Shows like *CSI* definitely raise the expectations of jurors.	☐	☐
3. *CSI* realistically depicts how criminal investigations are conducted.	☐	☐
4. Some investigators now conduct tests only to impress juries.	☐	☐

6 MUSICIANS AND MUSIC

LESSON A ▶ *A world of music*

1 GRAMMAR

Choose the words that best complete the sentences.

1. Generally, the more well known a singer is, the (more) / less money he or she makes.
2. The less publicity a musician gets, the *easier / harder* it is to make a living.
3. Some say the earlier you expose children to classical music, the *more / fewer* likely they are to excel in school.
4. The more relaxing the music, the *faster / slower* I fall asleep.
5. In my opinion, the more you listen to some song lyrics, the *fewer / less* you are able to understand them.
6. For some musicians, the more people gossip about their private lives, the *better / sooner*!

2 GRAMMAR

Complete the interview with the words from the box.

better	less	longer	more	sooner

Lily: When did you realize you wanted to be a guitarist?

Shane: I was 10 years old. My brother was taking guitar lessons, and the more I heard him practice, the (1) _____ **more** _____ I wanted to play guitar just as well.

Lily: Who were your biggest musical influences?

Shane: My biggest influence was Jack White. The more I listened to his music, the (2) _____ it got.

Lily: Jack White is great, but your music doesn't sound like his.

Shane: Yeah, I know. I realized that the more I listened to Jack White's music, the (3) _____ I wanted to sound like him. I wanted my own sound – something that made me unique.

Lily: You've certainly succeeded! What's next for you?

Shane: I'm moving to New York City. The (4) _____ I stay in Los Angeles, the more I realize I need a change.

Lily: Why is that?

Shane: I'd like to be part of a growing music scene, and apparently a lot is happening in New York.

Lily: When will you leave?

Shane: I'm not sure yet, but I think the (5) _____ I leave, the better.

3 VOCABULARY

Choose the adjectives that best describe your opinion of each kind of music. Then write a sentence explaining why.

1. pop (catchy / frenetic / monotonous)

   Successful pop music is catchy. The best pop songs are
   hard to forget—even years later.

2. classical (exhilarating / haunting / soothing)

   _____

   _____

3. jazz (evocative / mellow / frenetic)

   _____

   _____

4. hip-hop (catchy / evocative / monotonous)

   _____

   _____

5. folk (haunting / soothing / catchy)

   _____

   _____

6. rock (monotonous / exhilarating / frenetic)

   _____

   _____

4 GRAMMAR

Complete the sentences with double comparatives and your own ideas to make them true for you.

1. The _____*louder*_____ the music, the _____*more*_____ I like it.

2. The _____ the lyrics of a song, the more likely I am to

   _____.

3. The _____ the music, the _____ I find it.

4. The _____ a musician's reputation, the _____
   I am to go to his or her concerts.

5. The _____ a piece of music, the more difficult it is to

   _____.

6. The _____ musicians use _____ in their songs,
   the less I enjoy them.

WRITING

A Read the characteristics of listening to live music and listening to recorded music. Then put them under the correct heading below.

You listen with many other people.	You can't adjust the volume.
Sometimes you hear music you don't like.	You can listen to a song over and over.
You can't see the musicians while you listen.	You can listen to any kind of music you're in the mood for.
You can sing along with your favorite songs.	You can listen to music in any order you'd like.
You can adjust the volume.	You can turn off or skip songs you don't like.
You can hear music by well-known artists.	You can listen only when musicians are playing on stage.

Live music

_____

_____

_____

_____

_____

_____

Recorded music

_____

_____

_____

_____

_____

_____

Live music and recorded music

_____

_____

_____

_____

_____

_____

B What is your opinion of listening to live music versus listening to recorded music? Write a thesis statement expressing your opinion on the subject.

_____

_____

_____

C Now write a compare-and-contrast essay. Include your thesis statement in the introduction, two paragraphs describing the similarities and differences, and a conclusion restating your point of view.

1 VOCABULARY

Correct the underlined mistake in each sentence with one of the words in the box.
Some words will be used more than once.

be	break	get	make	pay

1. Most musicians must <u>break</u> their dues before they become successful. _____*pay*_____
2. After retiring in 2012, my favorite band is planning to <u>get</u> a comeback. _____
3. Gotye's latest song is going to <u>pay</u> a big hit. _____
4. I want to be a singer. What advice do you have to <u>make</u> into the business? _____
5. Many famous singers <u>be</u> their big break as contestants on *American Idol*. _____
6. It was so difficult for Jay-Z to <u>break</u> his foot in the door that he started his own record label. _____
7. The first time I heard Madonna, I knew she wouldn't <u>pay</u> a one-hit wonder. _____
8. While some musicians may be talented and work hard, they might never <u>get</u> a name for themselves in the music industry. _____

2 GRAMMAR

Complete these conversations. Use the verbs in parentheses and *would* or *will*.

1. Kim: I used to listen to all kinds of music when I was younger.
   Ron: Not me! When I was young, I _____*would listen*_____ (listen) only to rock music.

2. Dan: You play the guitar so well. How often do you practice?
   Sally: I practice all the time. In fact, I _____ (practice) four to five hours a day, depending on my schedule.

3. Mario: What do you like to do in your spare time?
   Kate: I don't have much spare time, but when I do, I _____ (go) to jazz clubs and concerts. Music helps me relax.

4. Fay: I can't believe the lead singer of the band we saw spent so much time after the show talking with his fans and signing autographs.
   Amy: I know. Most singers these days _____ (not spend) any time with their fans, let alone sign autographs!

5. Paula: When I was a teenager, I loved to listen to music that was really loud.
   Diana: Me, too. In fact, I _____ (turn up) my stereo as loud as I could. Unfortunately, now I have hearing problems.

6. Rob: I just heard my favorite Beatles song on the radio.
   Lori: I love the Beatles. In college I _____ (listen) to them every day.

3 GRAMMAR

Read the sentences about a band. Then choose the sentences that incorrectly use *will* or *would* and correct them.

☑ 1. When the band comes onstage, the crowd would scream.
When the band comes onstage, the crowd will scream.

☐ 2. Before the band got so popular, it will never sell out a concert in such a short time.
_____

☐ 3. Years ago, only bands with great musicianship would make it big.
_____

☐ 4. When the guitarist was young, he would practice in front of a mirror.
_____

☐ 5. In the past, the band will play only hard rock songs.
_____

☐ 6. Although the band used to sign autographs after a show, these days, security guards would not let fans backstage.
_____

4 GRAMMAR

Which music habits were or were not true for you in the past?
Which are or are not true now? Write sentences with *would* or *will*.

1. listen to a song over and over again
When I find a song I really love, I will listen to it over
and over again.

2. listen to very loud music
_____
_____

3. spend a lot of money downloading music
_____
_____

4. take music lessons
_____
_____

5. travel long distances to see live concerts of favorite bands
_____

6. argue with family members about musical tastes
_____

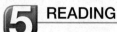

A Read the article quickly. What do you think the root *neuro-* in words such as *neurobiologist* means?

Music May Someday
Help Repair the Brain

The music that makes the foot tap, the fingers snap, and the pulse quicken stirs the brain at its most fundamental levels, suggesting that scientists one day may be able to retune damaged minds by exploiting rhythm, harmony, and melody, according to some research.

"Undeniably, there is a biology of music," said neurobiologist Mark Jude Tramo. "Music is biologically part of human life, just as music is aesthetically part of human life."

Researchers found that the brain:

■ Responds directly to harmony. Neuroscientists discovered that different parts of the brain involved in emotion are activated depending on whether the music is pleasant or unpleasant.

■ Interprets written music in an area on its right side. That region corresponds to an area on the opposite side of the brain known to handle written words and letters. So, researchers uncovered an anatomical link between music and language.

■ Grows in response to musical training. In a study of classically trained musicians, researchers discovered that male musicians have significantly larger brains than men who have not had extensive musical training. Although no similar increase has been found in female musicians, this might be explained by insufficient and inconclusive research.

Overall, music seems to involve the brain at almost every level, and researchers are already looking for ways to harness the power of music to change the brain. Research also suggests that music may play some role in enhancing intelligence. Indeed, so seductive is the possibility that music can boost a child's IQ that some politicians have lobbied for children to be exposed regularly to Mozart sonatas, although such research has yet to be confirmed.

The scientists said the research could help the clinical practice of neurology, including cognitive rehabilitation. As a therapeutic tool, for example, some doctors already use music to help rehabilitate stroke patients. Surprisingly, some stroke patients who have lost their ability to speak retain their ability to sing, and that opens an avenue for therapists to retrain the brain's speech centers.

B Read the statements. Are they supported by the information in the article? Choose yes or no.

	Yes	No
1. Different areas of the brain respond to music.	☐	☐
2. The brains of classically trained male musicians grow larger than the brains of nonmusical males.	☐	☐
3. Different pieces of classical music affect the brain in different ways.	☐	☐
4. Children who listen to Mozart sonatas develop higher intelligence than those who do not have exposure to this music.	☐	☐
5. Some stroke victims who are unable to speak are able to sing.	☐	☐

7 CHANGING TIMES

LESSON A ▶ *Lifestyles in transition*

1 GRAMMAR

Underline the relative pronouns in this announcement.

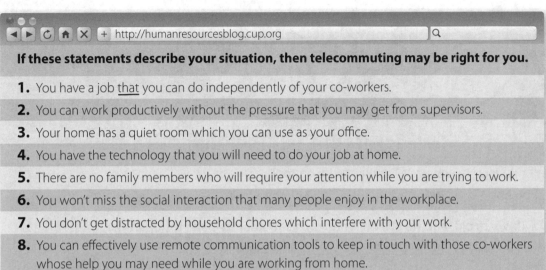

If these statements describe your situation, then telecommuting may be right for you.

1. You have a job <u>that</u> you can do independently of your co-workers.
2. You can work productively without the pressure that you may get from supervisors.
3. Your home has a quiet room which you can use as your office.
4. You have the technology that you will need to do your job at home.
5. There are no family members who will require your attention while you are trying to work.
6. You won't miss the social interaction that many people enjoy in the workplace.
7. You don't get distracted by household chores which interfere with your work.
8. You can effectively use remote communication tools to keep in touch with those co-workers whose help you may need while you are working from home.

See your Human Resources representative for details about our telecommuting policy.

2 GRAMMAR

Combine these sentences using a relative pronoun. Then write *O* if the relative pronoun is optional and *R* if the relative pronoun is required.

__O__ 1. Physical fitness is an important goal. A lot of people try to achieve this goal.
     Physical fitness is an important goal that a lot of people try to achieve.

_____ 2. Many people stay fit. These people find the time to work out regularly at a gym.
     _____

_____ 3. For the best results, it's important to find a gym. You like this gym.
     _____

_____ 4. It may be a good idea to hire a trainer. A trainer can work with you privately.
     _____

_____ 5. Your trainer can give you advice. The advice can help you avoid injuries.
     _____

_____ 6. If you get bored at the gym, try bringing some music. You can listen to the music while you exercise.
     _____

3 VOCABULARY

Use the words in the box to complete these conversations.

consistent	illogical	immature	inconsiderate	indecisive	responsible

1. A: I can't make up my mind. Which tie looks better?

   B: Don't be so _____*indecisive*_____. Just choose one.

2. A: Jim is 40 years old, and he still depends on his mother to clean his apartment.

   B: I know. He really is _____ in some ways.

3. A: Why did Meredith buy such a large car with gas prices so high?

   B: I know it seems _____, but she needs a big car for her job.

4. A: Doesn't Allison look great? What is she doing?

   B: She's been eating better and exercising on a _____ basis.

5. A: Why does Nate play his music so loudly when he knows we have to study?

   B: I don't know. He's so _____ of our needs. He just doesn't care.

6. A: I really like the new waiter you hired. He's very dependable.

   B: Yes, he is. Even though he's young, he's quite _____.

4 GRAMMAR

Use relative clauses and your own ideas to complete these sentences.

1. I have always admired people *who are good at organizing their time.*

2. I've always thought that I would enjoy a lifestyle _____

3. Parents _____ should be greatly admired.

4. These days many people want jobs _____

5. Finding enough time to spend with family and friends is a problem _____

   _____

A Read this composition about a personal experience and answer the questions.

The family that eats together, stays together

I feel it is very important for families to have regular meals together. One of my most positive childhood memories was dinner with my parents and two sisters. As a result, last year I decided that my family would have dinner together three days a week. Because my husband and I both work, and our kids are busy with school activities, we found that we rarely had a chance to get together as a family. But we thought it would be possible for everyone to set aside three evenings a week for a sit-down dinner.

First, we tried setting three fixed days for our experiment – Mondays, Wednesdays, and Fridays. After a couple of weeks of trying this plan, almost everyone was unhappy. Then my son had the idea of having everyone post his or her schedule for the week on the refrigerator every Sunday. I would choose the three best days, and those with scheduling conflicts . . .

For a while, the kids continued to resist the idea. They said they would rather spend the time with their friends or participate in sports or other activities. Gradually, though, they began to see these evenings together in a very positive way. We laughed a lot. We made vacation plans. We discussed each other's problems. After a couple of months, anyone who had to miss a family meal felt . . .

We all feel that we have been able to build much stronger relationships within the family than we had before. Of course, there are still disagreements, but we communicate better with each other now. The idea of having regular family meals together, which seemed difficult at first, has brought about many positive changes in our lives.

1. What is the thesis statement?

   _____

2. What is the focus of the second paragraph?

   _____

3. What is the focus of the third paragraph?

   _____

4. What sentence in the conclusion restates the thesis statement?

   _____

B Write a thesis statement for a composition about an important decision you have made recently.

_____

_____

C Now write your composition. Include an introduction, two paragraphs providing background information and details, and a conclusion.

1 GRAMMAR

Choose the expressions that best complete the sentences.

1. Cathy has decided to give up her high-powered job and do something more personally satisfying *(like)* / *as though* several of her friends have done.

2. Doesn't it seem *the way* / *as if* more people are trying to live a simpler life?

3. Elena feels *as* / *as though* she spends too much of her time commuting, so she is looking for work that she can do from home.

4. Today's kids don't have a lot of free time, *as* / *as if* we did when we were growing up, but they have many more opportunities.

5. Schools should offer music and art *as if* / *the way* they did when I was a student.

6. *As* / *As though* my aunt always says, "Make new friends, but keep your old ones."

7. Some days I feel *as if* / *the way* time passes too quickly.

8. *Like* / *As though* my mother before me, I serve a traditional dinner on special holidays for my family to enjoy.

2 VOCABULARY

Choose the expressions that are best exemplified by each situation.

a. anticipate a change	c. cope with change	e. resist change
b. bring about a change	d. go through a change	f. welcome a change

___e___ 1. Sherri's friends want her to move to Los Angeles with them, but she keeps coming up with reasons why she shouldn't go.

_____ 2. Mr. Viera's ideas encouraged our company to find ways for employees to work more closely with other departments.

_____ 3. After being on a plane for eight hours, Eun-ju was happy to finally land in Hawaii and begin her vacation.

_____ 4. When Mark retired from his job, he started playing golf and volunteering at the food bank.

_____ 5. Our school is in the process of moving to a new building and revising the schedule, so it's a challenging time for everyone.

_____ 6. We've realized it's time to move to a bigger house. We plan to start looking for a new place next month.

3 GRAMMAR

Read each situation and answer the questions using *as if*, *as though*, *as*, or *the way*. Sometimes more than one answer is possible.

1. Cal used to look forward to going fishing with his sons every summer. Now, his sons don't have time to go anymore. How does Cal feel?

   He feels as if he has lost a
   family tradition.

2. Anna has moved from a small town to a big city. It's exciting, and she's meeting lots of new people and discovering many new activities. How does Anna feel?

   _____

   _____

3. Mia used to spend a lot of time with her grandmother. Since Mia moved away, she only sees her grandmother twice a year. How does Mia feel?

   _____

   _____

4. In his spare time, Chris took an art class and discovered he had a real talent. Now he's about to have his first show in a gallery. How does Chris feel?

   _____

   _____

4 GRAMMAR

Complete these sentences so that they are true for you. Use *as if*, *as though*, *as*, *the way*, and *like*.

1. I feel ___*as though social media*___ is changing the way I relate to my friends.

2. I don't feel _____

   _____ when I was younger.

3. These days I think many people act _____

4. I still _____

   _____ my family did years ago.

5. Some people my age talk _____

   _____

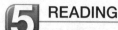

A Read the interview with Malcolm Gladwell about his book *The Tipping Point*. Find the words in boldface that match the definitions.

1. sudden increases in the occurence of something unpleasant _____*outbreaks*_____

2. the scientific study of epidemics _____

3. a comparison of two similar things _____

4. easily spread _____

THE TIPPING POINT: Q & A with Malcolm Gladwell

1 What is *The Tipping Point* about? It's a book about change. In particular, it's a book that presents a new way of understanding why change so often happens as quickly and as unexpectedly as it does. For example, why did crime drop so dramatically in New York City in the mid-1990s? How does a novel written by an unknown author end up as a national bestseller? Why is word-of-mouth so powerful? I think the answer to all these questions is the same. It's that behavior and messages and products sometimes behave just like **outbreaks** of infectious disease. They are social epidemics. *The Tipping Point* is an examination of the social epidemics that surround us.

2 Do you think the epidemic example is relevant for other kinds of change? I'm convinced that ideas and behaviors and new products move through a population very much like a disease does. This isn't just a metaphor. I'm talking about a very literal **analogy**. Ideas can be **contagious** in exactly the same way that a virus is.

3 How would you classify *The Tipping Point*? Is it a science book? I like to think of it as an intellectual adventure story. It draws from psychology and sociology and **epidemiology**, and uses examples from the worlds of business and education and fashion and media . . . all in aid of explaining a very common but mysterious phenomenon that we deal with every day.

4 What do you hope readers will take away from the book? One of the things I'd like to do is to show people how to start "positive" epidemics of their own. The virtue of an epidemic, after all, is that just a little input is enough to get it started, and it can spread very, very quickly. That makes it something of obvious and enormous interest to everyone, from educators trying to reach students, to businesses trying to spread the word about their product, or for that matter, to anyone who's trying to create a change with limited resources. By the end of the book, I think the reader will have a clear idea of what starting an epidemic actually takes. This is not an abstract, academic book. It's very practical. And it's very hopeful. It's brain software.

B Read the interview again. Choose the statements that are true according to the text.

☐ 1. *The Tipping Point* is a nonfiction book that draws from a number of different fields.

☐ 2. Gladwell believes that ideas, messages, and products spread in similar ways.

☐ 3. Before writing the book, Gladwell started a social epidemic of his own.

☐ 4. According to Gladwell, social epidemics do not occur very often.

☐ 5. Gladwell believes *The Tipping Point* should appeal to a wide range of readers.

☐ 6. *The Tipping Point* is not meant to be a book with practical applications.

8 CONSUMER CULTURE

LESSON A ▶ *What's new on the market?*

1 GRAMMAR

Underline the direct objects and circle the indirect objects in each sentence.

1. Some stores offer their (customers) frequent-buyer rewards as incentives to return.
2. Advertising is useful because it gives us information about improved products.
3. The salesperson recommended the latest headphones to me.
4. Someone had to explain the new printer to Daniel.
5. This GPS must have cost you a lot of money.
6. You should return those boots to the store if they're not comfortable.
7. Online auction sites offer collectors a great way to find the things they want.
8. I don't shop online often because I like to ask salespeople questions in person.

2 GRAMMAR

Unscramble the words to make sentences describing the woman's shopping experience.

1. the latest tablets / showed / the woman / the salesperson

   The salesperson showed the woman
   the latest tablets.

2. the woman / to / the GS5 model / recommended / the salesperson

   _____

3. her / the main features / he / described / to

   _____

4. him / the woman / the price / asked

   _____

5. the salesperson / the price / her / told

   _____

6. said / nothing / to / him / she / for a moment

   _____

7. a discount / offered / the salesperson / her

   _____

8. the money / the salesperson / she / to / gave

   _____

3 GRAMMAR

Use the words in the box to give advice about what to do in each situation. Include a direct and an indirect object in each sentence.

lend	mention	recommend	return	teach

1. Mai got a book from her brother for her birthday. She already has a copy of the book.
   Mai should return the book to the store and get one she doesn't have.

2. Ray and Pam want to go skiing with Kate, but Pam doesn't have enough money.
   _____

3. Ian speaks fluent Thai. His sister wants to learn Thai but doesn't want to take a class.
   _____

4. Jessica's favorite Italian restaurant is Luigi's. Her father wants to go out for Italian food but doesn't know any restaurants.
   _____

5. Max sold his car to a friend. The car uses a lot of oil, but he forgot to say anything about it.
   _____

4 VOCABULARY

Write a sentence about each situation using the expressions in the box.

bargain hunter	compulsive shopper	shopping spree
buyer's remorse	credit limit	window-shopping

1. Monica and Emil love to see what's on sale at their favorite stores. They can spend hours doing this without buying anything at all!
   Both Monica and Emil love to go window-shopping.

2. When Jeremy gets paid, he always buys things for himself whether he needs them or not. He often spends all of his money in one day.
   _____

3. Mark never pays full price for anything. He always searches for the best price. He even goes to different parts of town to get a good deal.
   _____

4. Before her wedding, Anne and her mother went shopping for everything they would need for the wedding. They spent a lot of money and had a great time.
   _____

5. Jen bought an expensive pair of earrings today. She loved them at the store, but now that she's home, she feels guilty for spending so much money.
   _____

6. While Eric was on vacation, he used his credit card for everything. At the end of the trip, he tried to buy a present, but his card was denied.
   _____

WRITING

A For each opinion, choose the two examples or details that support it. Then write another sentence to support the opinion.

1. Using an online supermarket saves you time and money.
   - ☐ a. Groceries purchased online are delivered directly to your home.
   - ☐ b. There is less chance to make an impulse buy because you are not actually in the store.
   - ☐ c. Online supermarkets often offer exotic produce that is not available in local grocery stores.

   _____

   _____

2. There is little reason to buy a camera if you have one on your phone.
   - ☐ a. With the right apps, you can edit your photos on the phone and share them on social media.
   - ☐ b. A good camera will usually produce better images than a phone.
   - ☐ c. It's easy to forget to bring a camera, but you probably always have your phone with you.

   _____

   _____

3. Today's children are too materialistic.
   - ☐ a. Many children have more free time than they have ever had before.
   - ☐ b. They compete to have the coolest gadgets and the most expensive hobbies.
   - ☐ c. Parents complain that children only want money from them.

   _____

   _____

B Write a thesis statement about one of the opinions above or one of your own.

_____

_____

C Write a composition. Include your thesis statement in the first paragraph, and develop your opinion with examples and details in subsequent paragraphs.

GRAMMAR

Read the email from a customer to the manager of a supermarket. Underline the subjunctive verbs.

> Dear Manager,
>
> I saw the sales flier for your supermarket, and I felt it was imperative that I <u>write</u> you. All the food on sale this week is snack food or other highly processed foods. Although I buy these foods occasionally, I suggest that local and organic foods be on sale, too. It's crucial that people have the chance to buy affordable local foods, and I recommend that your supermarket start offering these items at better prices. I also propose that you offer a larger selection of fresh fruits and vegetables. Many people don't buy fresh foods because they are not easily available. I think it's essential that your customers get the chance to incorporate these foods into their meals.
>
> Thank you.
>
> Marcella Guzman

GRAMMAR

Use the words in parentheses to rewrite each sentence using the subjunctive.

1. People should learn how to block offensive ads on their devices. (it is important)
   It is important that people learn how to block offensive ads on their devices.

2. A health-conscious person should eat fast food only once or twice a month. (it is vital)

3. Parents should read reviews before their children see a movie. (it is essential)

4. The government must prevent students from dropping out of school. (we insist)

GRAMMAR

Complete these sentences with your own ideas.

1. If you are suspicious about an ad for a product, I suggest that *you go online and read some reviews of the product.*

2. If you find an ad offensive, I recommend that _____

3. If you think a particular product is good, I propose that _____

4. If you want to pursue a career in advertising, it is important that _____

VOCABULARY

What marketing strategies would you use for each product or business? Use the phrases in the box to write sentences explaining your decisions.

celebrity endorsements	coupon codes	a loyalty program	search-engine marketing
comparative marketing	free samples	product placement	word-of-mouth marketing

1. ice cream *I would use free samples*
   because everyone would taste the ice cream,
   and many people might like it so much
   they'd buy more.

2. an action movie _____

3. a new restaurant _____

4. sports equipment _____

5. a health club _____

6. electronics _____

A Read the article quickly. Which senses were the focus of the marketing strategies and experiments mentioned? Choose the correct answers.

☐ hearing ☐ sight ☐ smell ☐ taste ☐ touch

Sensory ploys and the scent of MARKETING

Global brands have become increasingly aware of the power of sight, smell, touch, and sound to influence purchasing behaviors.

A fast-food chain has trialed scents for use in its restaurants with the knowledge that this not only draws in customers but also improves their perception of their overall dining experience. A company that produces a popular deodorant for men has spent considerable sums perfecting the sound of its aerosol can to amplify its brand message of strength and effectiveness. This has led to a spray that is noticeably louder than their "female" deodorants.

A subtle scent or a particular sound can be just enough to awaken positive past associations or simply alter our other sensory perceptions. Charles Spence, professor of experimental psychology and a sensory consultant to brands, points to research conducted by a company about 15 years ago. The company discovered that by adding a fragrance to clothes, they were perceived by users as whiter even when they weren't.

Other tricks, such as using high-pitched music, can drive people toward the top of a website, Professor Spence says. Meanwhile, by simply changing the background color on their website, companies can increase trustworthiness. This is of particular value, for example, when asking customers to enter their credit card details.

But brands do not always get it right. Back in 2008, one food company knew that consumers responded positively not only to crunchier chips but also to noisier packaging. So it introduced new noisy packaging for one of its chips. It was so loud that it reached as high as 105 decibels, louder than a lawnmower or food processor. Two years later, the company withdrew the packaging following widespread consumer complaints. There can be advantages in tapping into consumers' senses, but brands can clearly go too far.

B Read the article again. Choose the correct answer for each question.

1. What is this article mostly about?
   ☐ a. How marketing improves consumers' sensory experience.
   ☐ b. How to avoid being tricked by sensory marketing strategies.
   ☐ c. How marketing makes use of the senses to influence consumers.

2. Which of these statements is true according to the article?
   ☐ a. Sensory information doesn't have to be obvious to affect our perception of a product.
   ☐ b. Sensory information only triggers positive associations.
   ☐ c. One sense has no influence on how the other senses perceive a product.

3. Which of the following is **not** mentioned in the article?
   ☐ a. Particular scents can drive consumers into a restaurant.
   ☐ b. A white product is considered more reliable by customers.
   ☐ c. Packages that produce the wrong sound can drive customers away.

9 NATURE

LESSON A ▶ *Animals in our lives*

1 GRAMMAR

Complete these sentences using *whenever* or *wherever*.
If the time or place is specified, use *when* or *where*.

1. For some reason, _____*wherever*_____ I go with my pet snake, people get upset.

2. Many cats will rub against their owners' legs _____ they want to show affection.

3. Research indicates that _____ a person strokes an animal, his or her blood pressure goes down. Also, it's been argued that trained dogs should be present _____ there are people recovering from illnesses.

4. _____ I grew up, it wasn't common for people to have pets in their homes.

5. _____ I got my pet, I took on a serious responsibility. Being able to keep an animal healthy and fit depends on constant care and attention.

2 GRAMMAR

Rewrite the last sentence of each conversation with a sentence including a clause starting with *whenever* or *wherever*.

1. A: I'm going over to Chelsea's apartment. Would you like to come with me?
   B: No, I can't. She has a cat, and I'm allergic to them. Any time I'm around a cat, I start sneezing.
   Whenever I'm around a cat, I start sneezing.

2. A: Did you enjoy your visit to the rain forest preserve?
   B: I did. Everywhere I looked, there were amazing plants and animals.
   _____

3. A: What's wrong with your cat? She looks upset.
   B: She's just excited. She looks like that any time she sees a bird outside.
   _____

4. A: What kind of pet would you like to have?
   B: I'd love to get some fish. Any time I see fish swimming, I feel calm.
   _____

3 VOCABULARY

Write the correct word under each picture.

beak	fangs	fin	hooves	paws	tusks
claws	feather	gills	horns	tail	wing

1. _____*feather*_____

2. _____

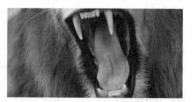

3. _____

4. _____

5. _____

6. _____

7. _____

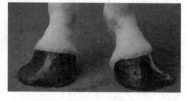

8. _____

9. _____

10. _____

11. _____

12. _____

4 GRAMMAR

Complete these sentences so that they are true for you.

1. Whenever I spend time with animals, _____

_____

2. When animals are kept in zoos, _____

_____

3. Wherever there are performances by animals, _____

_____

4. Wild animals should be kept where _____

_____

WRITING

A Read the thesis statements. Do the topic sentences belong in the composition? Choose yes or no.

	Yes	No
1. Thesis statement: Owning a pet has many health benefits.		
a. People who own pets often have better physical health than people who do not own pets.	☐	☐
b. People who own pets handle daily stresses better.	☐	☐
c. Pet owners often spend a lot of money on medicine for their pets.	☐	☐
d. People who have pets may be happier than other people.	☐	☐
2. Thesis statement: There are several effective ways to promote the survival of endangered animal species.		
a. Animals held in small enclosures often feel high levels of stress.	☐	☐
b. Conservation groups work to restore the natural habitats of endangered animals before reintroducing them to the wild.	☐	☐
c. Zoos are often successful at breeding endangered animals.	☐	☐
d. Hikers rarely spot endangered animals in the wild.	☐	☐
3. Thesis statement: Animal studies may lead to advances in technology.		
a. Spider web research could result in stronger buildings being built.	☐	☐
b. Learning more about how bats "see" in the dark may lead to new medical technologies.	☐	☐
c. Insects such as bees and ants live in highly structured societies.	☐	☐
d. Understanding how butterfly wings reflect light is inspiring engineers to create new types of computer screens.	☐	☐

B How are animals viewed in your culture? Write a thesis statement and topic sentences for three paragraphs.

Thesis statement: _____

_____

1. _____

2. _____

3. _____

C Now write a classification essay that includes your thesis statement in the introduction, three paragraphs corresponding to your topic sentences, and a conclusion.

1 GRAMMAR

Choose the words that best complete the sentences.

1. *Whatever / Whoever* has some free time this weekend should volunteer for the yearly beach cleanup.

2. Helen went to the woods to photograph *whatever / whoever* she could find for a project on medicinal plants.

3. The members of our surfing club are doing *whatever / whoever* they can to save enough for a trip to Hawaii.

4. I would never swim with sharks, but *whatever / whoever* does is very brave, in my opinion.

5. Can you tell me *whatever / whoever* you know about Professor Blake's research in the Arctic?

6. *Whatever / Whoever* has been dumping trash in the wildlife preserve should definitely be punished.

2 VOCABULARY

Complete the conversations with the correct idioms from the box.

a breath of fresh air	a walk in the park	the tip of the iceberg	set in stone
a drop in the ocean	as clear as mud	under the weather	up in the air

1. A: Do you understand these instructions?

   B: Not at all. They're _____ to me.

2. A: Are you feeling all right?

   B: Not really. I'm afraid I'm a little bit _____.

3. A: The new park director is full of great ideas!

   B: I know. She's _____ after working with the same people for so long.

4. A: I hear that the city spent way too much on the new waterfront park.

   B: Yes, but that's just _____. They overspent on many other projects, too.

5. A: Is it going to be difficult to raise money for the Save the Pandas campaign?

   B: I don't think so. They're such popular animals, it should be _____.

6. A: How closely do we have to follow the guidelines?

   B: They're not _____ yet, but let's keep them in mind while they're being finalized.

7. A: Have they decided who is going to speak at the biology convention in June?

   B: Not yet. It's still _____.

8. A: It's great that you're helping to save endangered owls.

   B: Unfortunately, it's just _____. There are many other animals that need help.

3 GRAMMAR

Do you agree or disagree with these statements? Respond to what the first speaker says.
Write sentences with *whoever* or *whatever*.

1. A: It's acceptable to build resorts in protected
      natural areas.

   B: *I disagree. We should do whatever we can*
      to protect natural areas.

2. A: People who drop litter in parks should pay very
      large fines.

   B: _____

   _____

BIRDS ONLY
Past This
Point

3. A: Everything governments usually do to protect
      endangered species is enough.

   B: _____

   _____

4. A: We should do everything we can to keep wild
      animals in their natural habitats.

   B: _____

   _____

5. A: People should never hike alone in unfamiliar forests.

   B: _____

   _____

4 GRAMMAR

Complete these sentences with ideas of your own. Use *whoever* or *whatever.*

1. *Whoever wants to have a real wilderness experience* should think about *trekking*
   in the Australian outback.

2. Whatever you need for your trip _____

   _____

3. _____

   must watch this nature documentary about _____

4. I do whatever I can _____

   _____

5. _____

   _____ will be amazed by the beautiful views.

5 READING

A Read the title and first paragraph of this story, and answer the questions.
Then read the rest of the story.

1. How well known is the fairy tale mentioned in the first paragraph? _____

2. What sentences indicate that the story will be true? _____

_____

A Fairy Tale Comes True

Every Bosnian child knows the story of a poor woman who caught a golden fish, released it, and in return gained wealth and happiness. It's a Balkan fairy tale, but it turned into reality for one poor family. "Whatever happened here is beyond good luck – it really is a fable," said Admir Malkoc.

In 1990, Smajo Malkoc returned from working in Austria to Jezero, a village surrounding a lake, in the former Yugoslavia. He had an unusual gift for his teenaged sons Dzevad and Catib: an aquarium with two goldfish.

Two years passed. War broke out, and Smajo Malkoc was killed.

When his wife, Fehima, sneaked back into the destroyed village to bury her husband, she spotted the fish in the aquarium. She let them out into the nearby lake. "This way they might be more fortunate than us," she recalls thinking.

Fast-forward to 1995. Fehima returned with her sons to Jezero to find ruins. Eyes misting over, she turned toward the lake and glimpsed something strange. She came closer — and caught her breath.

"The whole lake was shining from the golden fish in it," she said. During the years of war and killing all around the lake, life underwater had flourished.

After their return, Fehima and her sons started feeding the fish and then selling them. Now, homes, bars, and coffee shops in the region have aquariums containing fish from Jezero.

The Malkoc house, rebuilt from ruins, is one of the biggest in the village. The family says it has enough money not to have to worry about the future.

Other residents are welcome to catch and sell the fish. But most leave that to the Malkocs. "They threw the fish into the lake," said a villager. "It's their miracle."

B Put the events in order. Write an *X* for events not mentioned or indicated in the story.

_____ a. Mrs. Malkoc put the fish in a lake.

_____ b. The war broke out and Mr. Malkoc was killed.

_____ c. The Malkoc family started taking care of the fish in the lake.

_____ d. The Malkocs opened an aquarium in the village.

_____ e. Mrs. Malkoc and her children returned to their home.

_1_ f. Mr. Malkoc worked in another country.

_____ g. People from the region started buying fish from the Malkocs.

_____ h. The Malkocs provided money for other villagers to rebuild their homes.

_____ i. Mr. Malkoc presented two goldfish to his children when he came home.

54 **UNIT 9** Nature

GRAMMAR

Choose the words or phrases that best complete the sentences.

1. Kyle (was giving) / *was being given* a presentation in front of the whole company for the first time in his life.

2. When he *introduced / was introduced* by the vice president of the company, she got his name wrong.

3. When Kyle turned on the projector, everyone saw a family photo instead of the presentation that *should have displayed / should have been displayed* on the screen.

4. He was so flustered that he *dropped / was dropped* his tablet on the floor.

5. When he picked up the tablet, it *wasn't working / wasn't being worked*.

6. Kyle knew a copy of the presentation *might have saved / might have been saved* on his manager's tablet, so he borrowed it.

7. In spite of the initial problems, the presentation went well, and Kyle's manager *has praised / has been praised* him for a job well done.

GRAMMAR

Rewrite each sentence using the passive voice. Do not include the agent.

1. After the soccer team won the championship, the coach thanked the players.
   The players were thanked after the soccer team won the championship.

2. People have told me that I have good presentation skills.

   _____

3. Schools should teach foreign languages beginning in elementary school.

   _____

4. My college is awarding a new prize to the best debate team.

   _____

5. Someone is going to interview the best-selling author on TV tonight.

   _____

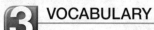

3 VOCABULARY

Rewrite the sentences by replacing the underlined words with a word or phrase from the box. If there are two possible answers, write both of them.

first of all	in addition	likewise	next	to begin	yet
furthermore	in conclusion	nevertheless	similarly	to sum up	

1. <u>To start with</u>, welcome to our seminar, "Giving Your Best Presentation."

   To begin / First of all, welcome to our seminar, "Giving Your Best Presentation."

2. When faced with giving a presentation, many people don't know where to start. <u>Also</u>, many of us get very nervous just thinking about presenting our ideas in public.

   _____

3. So, here are a few tips. <u>Before anything else</u>, outline your ideas carefully.

   _____

4. Make sure you have all the visuals you need for your presentation. <u>However</u>, don't depend too much on pictures and charts – what you say is just as important.

   _____

5. Don't rush the preparation of your materials. <u>In the same manner</u>, give yourself plenty of time to become familiar with the information you want to communicate.

   _____

6. <u>Then</u> practice the presentation a couple of times to build your confidence.

   _____

7. <u>To conclude</u>, preparation, practice, and confidence are the keys to a successful presentation.

   _____

4 GRAMMAR

Complete the sentences with your own ideas. Use the passive.

1. _My best friend's team was awarded_ first prize in the university debate competition.

2. _____

   _____ when he / she turned the radio up too loud in the car.

3. _____

   _____ he / she talks too much while watching movies.

4. _____

   _____ a speech at our school's graduation ceremony.

5. _____

   _____ for being one of the most generous people in our country.

5 WRITING

A Read the two positions about whether or not schools should focus on teaching students how to do research online. Then find the supporting reasons for each position, and write them on the lines below.

Positions

1. Since knowing how to do research online is essential for twenty-first century learners, it should be focused on in schools.

   _____

   _____

   _____

2. While knowing how to do research online is important for twenty-first century learners, it should not be a focus in schools.

   _____

   _____

   _____

Reasons

- Most students in the twenty-first century already have the necessary skills to do research online or can learn these skills on their own.
- The Internet is changing rapidly, and the skills students learn today may no longer be relevant in the near future.
- Most students would benefit from training on how and where to find reliable information online.
- Learning how to successfully do research online is as important to future studies and careers as learning subjects such as math and history is.
- Class time should be used for teaching more complex content and skills.
- Many students need guidance to learn how to distinguish trustworthy sources from unreliable ones.

B Which position is closer to your own? Write a persuasive composition to explain your point of view. Be sure to argue against the opposing view.

GRAMMAR

Choose the correct form of the verbs. Sometimes more than one answer is possible.

At first, most social media sites **(1)** *was* / *were* seen as a fun way to keep in touch with friends, share photos, and play games. But anyone who **(2)** *uses* / *use* one of these websites today can see that many more important things **(3)** *is* / *are* going on, and no one using these sites regularly **(4)** *is* / *are* able to ignore the fact that their uses are changing. A lot of people **(5)** *shares* / *share* political news and information, and new ideas can start and grow on these sites. Also, if someone **(6)** *needs* / *need* help after an accident or disaster, social media can be used to spread the word. In some instances, a majority of the money raised for emergency situations **(7)** *comes* / *come* through social media, and many volunteers can be brought together in a matter of hours. Of course, none of us **(8)** *puts* / *put* our social media account to such serious uses all of the time, but it is great to know that the possibility is there if we need it.

GRAMMAR

Read these results from a student survey. Then use the words in the box to make statements. If the verb can take both singular and plural forms, write them both.

Why do you study a **foreign language**?	Percentage of students
1. I need to know the language to get a better job. ⟶	85%
2. I want to be able to speak the language when I travel. ⟶	100%
3. I have to study the language because it's a required subject. ⟶	30%
4. I need to be able to read literature in the language. ⟶	0%
5. I study the language because I enjoy it. ⟶	50%

all	half	majority	minority	none

1. need to know the language to get a better job

   A majority of the students needs/need to know the language to get a better job.

2. want to be able to speak the language when they travel

   _____

3. have to study the language because it's a required subject

   _____

4. need to be able to read literature in the language

   _____

5. study the language because they enjoy it

   _____

3 VOCABULARY

Complete the conversations by using the correct form of the expressions in the box.
Make any necessary changes to the expressions.

have a sharp tongue
have a way with words
love to hear oneself talk
stick to the point
talk behind someone's back
talk someone into something
talk someone's ear off

1. A: I really liked what Justin said about working together as a team.

   B: I agree. It was very inspiring. He really _*has a way with words*_.

2. A: Did Peter say anything about me after I left?

   B: No. He'd never _____. He'd tell you directly.

3. A: Did you tell Lisa about our plans for her birthday?

   B: I tried to, but she just kept _____ about her problems
   with her car.

4. A: Ms. Jones read my report and said awful things about it.

   B: Well, she _____, but she's also very perceptive.
   Just try to focus on what she's saying about your work.

5. A: I know you want to continue discussing the report, but I'd like to talk about
   my new customer.

   B: Let's _____. We can talk about that later.

6. A: That meeting was so long! I thought Bob would never stop talking!

   B: He sure _____, doesn't he?

7. A: Are you going to the company picnic this weekend?

   B: Well, I wasn't planning to, but Kelly convinced me to go. She knows how to
   _____ I don't want to do!

4 GRAMMAR

Complete these sentences with your own ideas. Use verbs in the present.

1. Each language in the world _*is unique.*_ _____

2. All bilingual people _____

3. Every one of my classmates _____

4. The majority of celebrities _____

A Read the article. Find the words in boldface that match these definitions.

1. form an idea of ___conceptualize___   4. only _____

2. researches _____   5. indicate _____

3. incredible _____   6. native _____

Does the language you speak change the way you think?

Do people who speak different languages actually think differently, or are the 7,000 languages in the world just different means for expressing a universal human way of thinking? To answer that question, linguist Lera Boroditsky **surveys** differences between languages across a number of fundamental categories, including how speakers of different languages **conceptualize** space and time, and how they think about gender.

Regarding spatial orientation, she says, "There are some languages that don't use words like 'left' and 'right.' Instead, everything in the language is laid out in absolute space. That means you have to say things like, 'There is an ant on your northwest leg.'"

The language of the Kuuk Thaayore, an **aboriginal** group in Australia, works like that. Boroditsky's research has shown that the unique way they think about space also affects the way they think about time. Whereas English speakers tend to conceptualize time as running from left to right, the Kuuk Thaayore visualize it from east to west.

Then there is gender. Some languages, like Hebrew, **mark** gender for both people and objects, while Finnish has almost no gender information at all. "English," says Boroditsky, "is somewhere in the middle."

Boroditsky explains the degree to which a language emphasizes gender in its grammatical structure actually affects the way speakers think. She cites a study by Alexander Guiora, who looked at kids learning Hebrew, Finnish, and English as their first language. He asked them, "Are you a boy or a girl?" and had all kinds of clever ways of figuring out how aware they were of their gender. What he found was that kids in these three groups figure it out at different rates. The Hebrew-speaking kids got it first, then the English-speaking kids, and the Finnish-speaking kids last.

These are just a few examples of the **mind-bending** differences Boroditsky has found. She also talks about how the language you speak affects the way you look at colors and changes the way you think about the relationship between cause and effect.

As to the main question – does language affect the way people think – Boroditsky's answer is a clear "yes." At the same time, she allows that language is not the **sole** determinant of thought. "Language shapes thought, and also the way that we think importantly shapes the way we talk," she says, "and aspects of culture importantly shape aspects of language. It's a bi-directional cycle."

B Are the statements true (*T*), false (*F*), or is the information not given (*NG*) in the article? Write the correct letters.

_____ 1. Boroditsky believes that language does affect thinking.

_____ 2. All languages indicate gender in the same way.

_____ 3. Most of the aboriginal languages in Australia conceptualize space and time in similar ways.

_____ 4. Boroditsky believes that language is not the only thing that influences thought.

11 EXCEPTIONAL PEOPLE

LESSON A ▶ *High achievers*

1 VOCABULARY

Choose the words that best complete the sentences.

1. The (coolheaded) / *soft-hearted* athlete was able to score despite the noisy crowd.

2. I'm so *absent-minded* / *hardheaded* that, after staying up late to finish my paper on time, I forgot to bring it to class!

3. Sam is the kindest and most *cold-blooded* / *warm-hearted* guy I know.

4. Although Emily appears to be silly and *narrow-minded* / *empty-headed,* she's actually quite intelligent.

5. Ethan is *hardheaded* / *hot-blooded.* Once he makes up his mind, he doesn't change.

6. I hope Zach is *cold-hearted* / *open-minded* about our idea. He isn't always willing to consider new approaches to solving problems.

7. My cousins are so *narrow-minded* / *soft-hearted* when it comes to music. They won't listen to anything except jazz.

8. The *cold-hearted* / *absent-minded* killer was sentenced to life in prison.

2 GRAMMAR

Rewrite these sentences using compound adjectives to replace the words in boldface. Sometimes more than one answer is possible.

1. The famous conductor is **recognized by many people**.
   The famous conductor is widely recognized.

2. In my opinion, the politician's speech was **too long**.
   _____

3. Nicole is a model **with curly hair and brown eyes**.
   _____

4. Alyssa is a **very relaxed** boss. She lets employees choose their hours.
   _____

5. Maxwell's is not a restaurant **that many people know about**.
   _____

6. Dr. Kendall's lectures really **make us think about things**.
   _____

7. Katy made a good impression at the interview because she was **dressed so well**.
   _____

What qualities should these people have? Write a sentence using two compound adjectives.

elementary school teacher

1. *An elementary school teacher should be kind-hearted and well educated.*

mountain climber

2. _____

_____

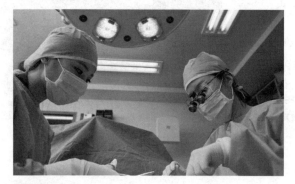

surgeon

3. _____

_____

_____

judge

4. _____

_____

_____

salesperson

5. _____

_____

_____

soccer player

6. _____

_____

_____

A Read this biographical profile of composer and conductor Leonard Bernstein. Answer the questions below.

LEONARD BERNSTEIN

LEONARD BERNSTEIN was perhaps the single greatest figure in American classical music in the twentieth century. Born in 1918 in Lawrence, Massachusetts, he studied piano as a child in Boston. **❶** Upon his graduation from Harvard University in 1939, he moved to Philadelphia to study at the Curtis Institute. **❷** By the time Bernstein finished his training, he was widely respected as a major talent in the music world. **❸**

In 1943, Bernstein became the assistant conductor of the New York Philharmonic. One night, he was asked to substitute for a conductor who was sick. This was a particularly difficult concert, but Bernstein performed brilliantly and was a great success. **❹** Over the next 15 years, he held conducting positions in several of the great orchestras of the world, and he performed as a guest conductor with many others. His work included both live concerts and recordings. **❺**

In 1958, Bernstein became the music director of the New York Philharmonic. That same year, he started a series of televised programs called *Young People's Concerts*, designed to teach children an appreciation for great music. At the Philharmonic, Bernstein was a very popular conductor. He brought new music to the orchestra and revitalized older music that hadn't been played for some time.

❻ Bernstein died in New York City in 1990. He conducted and composed music up until the time of his death. Through his lifetime of conducting, composing, teaching, and helping people understand music, he left a great gift to the world.

1. In what year did Leonard Bernstein leave Harvard University? _____

2. How long did Bernstein conduct orchestras all over the world before he became the music director of the New York Philharmonic? _____

3. In what year did Bernstein start *Young People's Concerts*? _____

B There are six numbered circles in the biographical profile. Find where each of the following sentences should go, and write the number of the circle next to the sentence.

_____ a. In 1969, Bernstein left the New York Philharmonic and spent the remaining years of his life composing a wide variety of music, conducting all over the world, and teaching young musicians.

_____ b. At 17, he entered Harvard University, where he studied composition.

_____ c. During his years there, he spent his summers at the Boston Symphony Orchestra's institute at Tanglewood, where he studied with the conductor Serge Koussevitzky.

C Choose someone you admire who has made a difference in people's lives. Research the key facts of the person's life, and write a biographical profile with an introduction and at least two other paragraphs.

1 GRAMMAR

Read the text and underline the superlative compound adjectives.

Without a doubt, <u>my most fondly remembered</u> teacher is Mr. Hill, my college French professor. He was the most kind-hearted man, and he always showed concern for his students. He went out of his way to make us feel comfortable in class, so we never felt too nervous or anxious to participate. He was the hardest-working teacher I've ever had, and he would always come up with creative ways to help us understand the most difficult lessons. Mr. Hill truly loved French culture, so the cultural lessons were the most thought-provoking of all my classes. He made me feel that I was looking through a window into another world, and he made me want to be a part of that world. I'm afraid I don't remember much French now – it's not the most easily retained language, especially if you don't use it often – but I did learn how great a teacher can be and how rewarding it can be to learn about another culture.

2 GRAMMAR

Read these conversations and fill in the blank with the superlative form of the adjectives in parentheses.

1. **Kay:** What did you think about the president's speech?

   Mindy: I thought it was ___*the most thought-provoking*___ (thought-provoking) speech she's ever given.

2. **Sung:** Don't you think Tom is a good cook?

   Nate: Definitely. His paella was _____ (great-tasting) dish I've had in a long time!

3. **Oscar:** What did you think of the lead actor's performance in the movie we saw last night?

   Valerie: I thought he was terrific. He gave one of _____ (heartbreakingly convincing) performances in the movie.

4. **Rich:** Have you seen the video of the singing dog?

   Linda: No, I haven't. But I've heard that it's _____ (widely downloaded) clip of the week.

5. **Tai:** Cory is always so kind to people!

   Sarah: I agree. He's probably _____ (warm-hearted) person I've ever met.

6. **Brad:** How was your trip to Morocco? Were you able to visit the desert?

   Nora: Oh, I was. It was one of _____ (breathtakingly beautiful) things I saw on my entire trip!

3 VOCABULARY

Correct the underlined mistake in each sentence with one of the words in the box. Some words will be used more than once.

after	on	to	through	with

1. I always look <u>through</u> my older sister for fashion advice. _____*to*_____

2. I know coping with a broken arm is difficult, but just be patient and you'll get <u>after</u> it. _____

3. I'm not sure who to side <u>to</u> in this argument! You both have valid points. _____

4. Many middle-aged people not only look <u>with</u> their children, but they take care of their elderly parents at the same time. _____

5. Who do you take <u>through</u> more, your mother or your father? _____

6. I have very high expectations for myself, and I get frustrated when I don't live up <u>on</u> them. _____

7. Excuse me while I check <u>after</u> the baby. I think I just heard her cry. _____

8. If you don't face up <u>with</u> your problems soon, they'll only get worse. _____

4 GRAMMAR

Use the cues to write sentences that are true for you. Use superlative compound adjectives in your sentences.

1. incredibly talented actress I can think of

   The most incredibly talented actress I can think
   of is Scarlett Johansson.

2. action-packed movie I've ever seen

   _____

   _____

3. time-saving invention I use

   _____

   _____

4. easily learned subject I've studied

   _____

   _____

5. well-intentioned person I've met

   _____

   _____

6. physically demanding sport I know

   _____

   _____

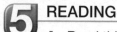

A Read this article about the Awesome Foundation. Choose the adjectives that best describe the organization.

☐ 1. old-fashioned   ☐ 3. highly structured   ☐ 5. nontraditional

☐ 2. loosely organized   ☐ 4. crowdsourced   ☐ 6. widespread

TINY GRANTS KEEP "awesome" IDEAS COMING

It was down to two finalists: a woman who wanted to buy a couple of goats to rent out as urban lawnmowers, and a sculptor who wanted to buy a portable welder so he could go around and fix his city. They were both awesome ideas, the trustees agreed, but only one of them could win money that month. And so they had to ask the ultimate question: Which idea was more awesome?

This is the basic premise behind the Awesome Foundation, which is not an actual foundation. It is more like a support group for good ideas. It began in Cambridge, Massachusetts, in 2009, when a group of tech-savvy twenty-somethings, frustrated by the bureaucracy of traditional funding, got together and, in essence, said, "You know what would be awesome? If there were an organization that gave you money if you had an awesome idea." Then they became that organization, loosely.

It works like this: Ten trustees each kick in $100 a month, and together they review the submissions. The winner is given $1,000 for the project, with no strings attached.

The idea is so simple that it has multiplied organically and become a new nonprofit model for the crowdsourcing generation. Today there are more than 20 chapters around the world. Anyone can start one, and the only real rule is that there is no definition for "awesome." That's for each trustee to decide.

The concept of a small grant, handed out by individuals, means the idea has a built-in lightness, according to Tim Hwang, who conceived of the Awesome Foundation shortly after he graduated from college. But there is a recurring bent toward socially conscious public projects. Christina Xu, one of the original trustees who had become frustrated with the failings of traditional nonprofits, says that she "realized maybe the Awesome Foundation was an answer" to that problem.

That may be a reach, but it's indicative of what attracts people to the Awesome Foundation – the belief that ordinary people can create positive change outside of the establishment.

In the end, the trustees unanimously chose the sculptor. They had questions about the goats, but there was no question that the sculptor's idea was awesome.

B Choose the statements that can be confirmed in the article.

☐ 1. Trustees generally fund Awesome awards with their own money.

☐ 2. Traditional nonprofit organizations admire the foundation's work.

☐ 3. There are no rules on who can set up a branch of the Awesome Foundation in a new city.

☐ 4. The foundation has funded thousands of projects around the world.

☐ 5. The foundation consciously avoids strictly defining what should be considered "awesome."

12 BUSINESS MATTERS

LESSON A ▶ *Entrepreneurs*

 VOCABULARY

Choose the words that best complete the sentences.

1. I would rather work *around* / *for* a boss who is organized and strict than a boss who is disorganized and nice.

2. Janelle worked *off* / *on* some of her debt to her cousin by designing and managing the website for his business.

3. Showing up late for appointments can work *against* / *toward* you if you are trying to start a new business.

4. If we don't find a way to work *toward* / *around* this problem, we'll never make our deadline.

5. The more people we have working *for* / *on* the report, the faster we'll get it done.

6. Jesse is working *off* / *toward* a degree in marketing and finance.

 GRAMMAR

Read each sentence and then answer the questions with *yes* or *no.*

Had Natalie not lost her job at a bakery, she would never have considered starting her own business.

1. Did Natalie lose her job at the bakery? _____*Yes*_____

2. Did she consider starting her own business? _____

Should Natalie's business continue to grow, she might hire another baker.

3. Is Natalie's business growing? _____

4. Has she hired another baker yet? _____

Had Natalie raised a large family, she might not have been able to spend a lot of time developing her business.

5. Was she able to spend a lot of time developing the business? _____

6. Did she raise a large family? _____

Natalie's Cookies might not have become the best-selling cookies in the city had she not worked so hard.

7. Did Natalie's Cookies become the best-selling cookies in the city? _____

8. Did Natalie work hard? _____

③ GRAMMAR

Complete the sentence for each situation using a conditional clause with *Had . . . not . . . .*

1. __*Had*__ the woman __*not answered the ad*__, she'd never have become a veterinary assistant.

2. _____ the couple _____, they wouldn't have had so many kittens at home.

3. _____ the man _____, he wouldn't have won first prize.

4. _____ the woman _____, she wouldn't have started her own business.

5. _____ the man _____, he would never have been served.

6. _____ the woman _____, she wouldn't have bought her new laptop.

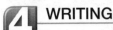

WRITING

A Read this formal letter. Three sentences do not belong because they are too personal or irrelevant. One has already been crossed out. Cross out the other two.

JD 85 SUN ROAD
PHOENIX, AZ 85051

June 7, 2014

Ms. Rosa Marquez
4226 E. 22nd St.
Phoenix, AZ 85016

Dear Ms. Marquez:

I am writing in response to the advertisement for a social media marketer in last week's edition of *Career Focus E-News Digest*. I am very interested in the position and am enclosing my résumé for your consideration. ~~It is very kind of you to read this letter.~~

I believe you will find that I meet all of the qualifications that you specify. In fact, you have probably never had a candidate as qualified as I am! I have had two years of experience as a social media marketing intern at a major nonprofit. Although this was an unpaid position, it gave me valuable experience in managing social media accounts, creating content, and working with analytics.

Additionally, I enjoy working as part of a team and am very good with people. None of my current colleagues wants me to leave.

I would appreciate the opportunity to discuss this position with you in person. I look forward to hearing from you at your convenience.

Sincerely,

James Ditzler

James Ditzler

B Imagine a job that you would be interested in having. Make notes on the following.

Why you want the position:

_____

_____

Your experience:

_____

_____

Why you should be considered:

_____

_____

C Use your notes to write a formal letter applying for the job you are interested in.

GRAMMAR

Choose the expressions that best complete the sentences.

1. (*Assuming that*)/ *Provided that* I were required to travel for a job, I would turn it down because I don't like to fly.

2. *On the condition that / Whether or not* we continued to get more business, we would have to move to bigger offices anyway.

3. *Whether or not / Provided that* an applicant had the right job skills, I'd definitely hire him or her.

4. *Supposing that / Provided that* your boss wanted to transfer you to another department, how would you feel about it?

5. *Assuming that / Whether or not* you have a good reason to change jobs, I'd strongly recommend staying at your present company.

GRAMMAR

Respond to what the first speaker says in the conversations. Write sentences using the adverb clauses of condition provided.

1. A: If I were offered an interesting job that paid well, I would accept it. (provided that)

   B: *I would probably accept it, too, provided that the benefits were also good.*

2. A: If I had to commute to work on a daily basis, I would definitely do it. It can't be that much of an inconvenience. (on the condition that)

   B: _____

   _____

3. A: If I didn't receive a raise within the first year I worked at a job, I'd leave it and find a new job. (assuming that)

   B: _____

   _____

4. A: Under no circumstances would I ever accept a demotion. No one should move down in a company. (supposing that)

   B: _____

   _____

5. A: If my boss said something in a meeting that I strongly disagreed with, I would definitely speak up. (whether or not)

   B: _____

   _____

6. A: I think that it's OK to lend a family member a large amount of money in order to help them start a business. (provided that)

   B: _____

   _____

3 GRAMMAR

Under what conditions would you do or not do these things? Write sentences using the expressions in the box.

| assuming (that) | on the condition (that) | provided (that) | supposing (that) | whether or not |

1. take a pay cut

   I'd take a pay cut on the condition I were given
   more interesting projects at work.

2. work every weekend

   _____
   _____

3. agree to be transferred to a different country

   _____
   _____

4. work two jobs at the same time

   _____
   _____

5. quit your job and go back to school

   _____
   _____

4 VOCABULARY

Choose the quality that you consider to be the most important for each job.
Then write a sentence explaining why.

1. doctor (leadership ability / training)

   Training is most important for doctors because people's lives are in their hands.

2. artist (self-discipline / initiative)

   _____

3. politician (charisma / influence)

   _____

4. teacher (communication skills / leadership ability)

   _____

5. writer (initiative / training)

   _____

6. business executive (influence / leadership ability)

   _____

5 READING

A Read the article quickly and answer the questions.

1. What percentage of employees report being truly engaged in their work? _____

2. How many companies does the author say completely meet his criteria? _____

The Twelve Attributes of a
TRULY GREAT PLACE TO WORK

More than 100 studies have found that the most engaged employees – those who report they're fully invested in their jobs and committed to their employers – are significantly more productive, drive higher customer satisfaction, and outperform those who are less engaged. But only 20 percent of employees around the world report that they're fully engaged at work. So, what's the solution? The answer is that great employers must shift the focus from trying to get more out of people to investing more in them by addressing their four core needs – physical, emotional, mental, and spiritual – so they're freed, fueled, and inspired to bring the best of themselves to work every day.

Think for a moment about what would make you feel most excited to get to work in the morning and most loyal to your employer. The sort of company I have in mind would:

1 Commit to paying every employee a living wage. No employee working full time should receive a sum that falls below the poverty line.

2 Give all employees a stake in the company's success. If the company does well, all employees should share in the success in meaningful ways.

3 Design working environments that are safe, comfortable, and appealing to work in. In offices, include a range of physical spaces that allow for privacy, collaboration, and simply hanging out.

4 Provide healthy, high-quality food at the lowest possible prices.

5 Create places for employees to rest and renew during the course of the working day and encourage them to take intermittent breaks.

6 Offer a well-equipped gym and other facilities that encourage employees to move and stay fit.

7 Define clear and specific expectations for what success looks like in any given job. Then treat employees as adults by giving them as much autonomy as possible.

8 Institute two-way performance reviews so that employees not only receive regular feedback about how they're doing but also have the chance to provide feedback to their supervisors.

9 Hold leaders and managers accountable for treating all employees with respect and care.

10 Create policies that encourage employees to set aside time to focus without interruption on their most important priorities.

11 Provide employees with ongoing opportunities and incentives to learn, develop, and grow.

12 Stand for something. Create products, provide services, or serve causes that add value in the world, making it possible for employees to feel good about the companies for which they work.

I've yet to come across a company that meets the full range of their people's needs in all the ways I've described. How about you?

B Answer the following questions with information from the article.

1. What are some of the benefits of having engaged employees?

_____

2. According to the author, what are the four core needs of employees?

_____

3. How does the author think office environments can be made more appealing?

_____

4. According to the article, how does a two-way performance review work?

_____